D1614829

JANICE MORPHET AND
BEN CLIFFORD

REVIVING LOCAL AUTHORITY HOUSING DELIVERY

Challenging Austerity through Municipal
Entrepreneurialism

POLICY PRESS **SHORTS** RESEARCH

First published in Great Britain in 2021 by

Policy Press, an imprint of
Bristol University Press
University of Bristol
1–9 Old Park Hill
Bristol
BS2 8BB
UK
t: +44 (0)117 954 5940
e: bup-info@bristol.ac.uk

Details of international sales and distribution partners are available at
policy.bristoluniversitypress.co.uk

British Library Cataloguing in Publication Data
A catalogue record for this book is available from the British Library

ISBN 978-1-4473-5574-8 hardcover
ISBN 978-1-4473-5576-2 ePub
ISBN 978-1-4473-5575-5 ePdf

Cover design: Policy Press
Front cover image: Dennis Gilbert/View Pictures/Universal
Images Group via Getty Images
Bristol University Press and Policy Press use environmentally
responsible print partners.
Printed in Great Britain by CPI Group (UK) Ltd,
Croydon, CR0 4YY

Contents

List of figures and tables

Preface

Since 2010, local authorities in England have experienced a period of government austerity, which has placed them under considerable stress as they strive to continue to meet the needs of their communities. At the same time, there has been mounting pressure to support the delivery of housing in their areas and meet increasing levels of homelessness. While the focus of the Localism Act 2011 was on housing and neighbourhood planning, the first part gave local authorities some general powers of competence that allowed them to operate in the same way as private sector organisations. This offered some new opportunities to return to municipal entrepreneurialism and reminded local authorities of some of their existing powers for the provision of housing, development and energy. Gradually, while the government has been diverted by Brexit, councils have been finding new ways to deliver housing and beginning to act as patient investors. They have started with small projects and have gradually increased their activity to provide more independence for their long-term future. Now, there is a wider view emerging that the only way that the country will provide the number of homes that it needs will be to return to a major social housing programme.

We have been interested in understanding how these changes have been emerging and, through two research projects (one in 2017 and one in 2019), we have been able to hear at first hand local authorities' experiences and ambitions for their areas. We have heard how councillors want to take more control of the quality, range, type and tenure of the housing provided in their areas than what is offered through current mechanisms, particularly private developers operating through the planning system. Local authorities are aware of the risks but also see that these approaches give them potentially greater freedom in meeting their local needs over the longer term. These approaches are worth some reflection and have implications for the operation of the local state.

We have both had lives that are steeped in local and central government and the academy. The finishing touches to this book are being made as the COVID-19 pandemic changes all our lives. As the pandemic has illustrated, local government in England has been initially marginalised in the response but is, and should be, central to securing control of the disease. COVID-19 offers risks to local authorities, for example increased demand for services at the same time as income from commercial sources such as property rental and fees may fall. However, there may also be opportunities, for example councils being offered development sites and properties by the private sector.

This dichotomy of threat and opportunity reflects the research findings discussed in this book, which predate the pandemic, but result from the crisis of austerity seen over the past decade. This politically imposed austerity has threatened service provision and the very existence of some councils, and we do not seek to gloss over the many negative consequences it has had. However, against this backdrop, local authorities have slowly started to take action to try to address the twin crises of austerity and housing together. There is the potential for local authorities to have more independence from central government and greater confidence in their ability to shape their own destiny. This more positive potential future is not definite, but there are possibilities, as we consider in this book, particularly in relation to greater involvement in the direct provision of housing. There could be considerable opportunity if a reshaped local government were less dependent on central government initiatives forced through an over-reliance on ever-reducing central funding. The pandemic might do more to reinforce this and we look forward to seeing how local authorities develop in the future.

In producing this book, we would like to acknowledge the many others who have helped to bring the research projects we draw on, and the book itself, to fruition. In particular, Mike Hayes from the National Planning Forum and Tom Kenny from the Royal Town Planning Institute were the key links in the organisations that funded the 2017 research project and Tom Kenny for the 2019 research project. Numerous local authority officers and councillors participated in both projects and we are very grateful to them. Emily Watt at Policy Press has been a very supportive editor for the book project. Finally, Ben would like to acknowledge the Faculty of Architecture, Building and Planning at the University of Melbourne, which was hosting him as a visiting scholar when he undertook much of his share of the writing of this book while on sabbatical leave from the Bartlett School of Planning, UCL.

Janice Morphet and Ben Clifford
London, July 2020

ONE

Introduction: local government in England and the twin crises of austerity and housing

Introduction

Since 2010, English local government has been on the front line of the Conservative Party's austerity policy. Through the coalition government (2010–15), and then Prime Ministers Cameron, May and Johnson, English local authorities have had their budgets cut by 49.1% (NAO, 2018) in real terms. At the same time as government funding has been significantly reduced, their responsibilities have increased, including for public health (2012) and homelessness reduction (2017). The primary block of central government funding for local government, the Revenue Support Grant (RSG), was tapered to zero by 2020, the Westminster 'deal' culture has tied funding to Whitehall project menus (Sandford, 2020) and local housing delivery funding has been centralised to a government agency – Homes England – which primarily supports private sector housing development. Local authorities were partners with central government in the delivery of the welfare state.

They are now viewed by Whitehall as a sector to be managed and controlled. As we have seen in the response to COVID-19, public health and primary care have been replaced by a privatised pandemic (Monbiot, 2020).

Local authorities have responded to austerity and these additional duties in a number of ways. Based on research undertaken by the authors, this book discusses how local authorities are drawing on their powers, resources, cultures and experiences to find ways to meet these austerity challenges and to promote their financial security for the future. While Prime Minister Boris Johnson may have indicated that the austerity period 2010–20 has ended (Stone, 2020), local authorities have started to make their own preparations for the future, and considered the ways they can respond to the very real challenges of austerity and keep funding their vital work.

At the same time, there is commonly held to be a 'housing crisis' in England. Over recent years, the focus of central government has very much been on enabling and encouraging greater delivery of housing by the private sector as the apparent solution to this crisis. The local planning system has had its focus shifted to the provision of housing land for private developers, there has been planning deregulation and there are increasing concerns about the quality of the dwellings and the contribution they make to the places of the future. For a hundred years, until 1980, local authorities were synonymous with housing regulation and provision. They were the post-war peace-time landlords, providing new homes to replace those lost in war and much of the damp, overcrowded, rented inner-city housing that frequently was all that was available. Although it has been more than 40 years since Margaret Thatcher introduced a tenant's right to buy their council home in 1980, local communities remember and, in many cases, continue to expect that councils will be the main providers of housing in their communities. When offered the opportunity of easy homeownership, people found this attractive. It was an opportunity to invest in an asset that could eventually be passed on to their own children. However, when their children could not get on the housing ladder – to rent or buy – then why did the council not step in, as it had done before? Local authorities have always provided a local safety net against unwelcome change or unexpected events. As our research has found, there is an expectation of them from their local communities to provide housing now.

As we discuss in this book, that local expectation has been a significant motivation for councils of all sizes, locations and political majorities to re-engage in the direct provision of housing. Many have started in small ways. Councils have adopted different strategies that have suited their cultures and local needs. Some have developed their own expertise and expanded their range of delivery methods. Increasingly, councils are thinking of their role as a patient investor, with a long-term stake in their areas, providing stability for local communities and accumulating some resources to support them in the future.

How and why are local authorities making these shifts to provide housing? Do they provide local authorities with more freedom from government in one of the most centralised states in the Organisation for Economic Co-operation and Development (OECD) (OECD, 2017)? As this book demonstrates, local authorities are using the local provision of housing to meet multiple local social, economic and environmental objectives. They are now leading change, not waiting for developers to deliver. Government funding continues to be important for supporting local development but, as this book shows, local authorities are moving away from dependency to innovation and change. Direct engagement in housing delivery is not the whole answer for the future of local authorities in England trying to cope with austerity, but it is providing many with an active and more hopeful approach to facing the future. This book outlines our extensive research into how and why local authorities are providing housing again and explores the relationship between that and austerity.

We argue that there can and should be a positive role for local government in housing development and that some of the innovative approaches emerging in England over recent years offer some hope for the future against the bleak backdrop of austerity. Before turning to our own research, we explore the twin contexts of the austerity crisis and the housing crisis in this introductory chapter.

An age of crisis for the local state?

Crises and dealing with so-called 'wicked problems' are defining features of governance (Clarke and Stewart, 2003; Head, 2008). In England, the past decade has seen two challenging crises closely involving local government: the crisis of austerity – impacting local government finances and capacity – and the housing crisis (with housing delivery and management long seen as a core role for the local state, as we outline in Chapter Two).

In terms of austerity, Bailey et al (2015) characterise this as a crisis period for local government, with cuts to its funding more severe in pace and depth than seen at any point in at least the past 50 years. In the UK, local government has for decades been highly exposed to decisions of central government due to having one of the most centralised local government funding systems in the developed world, with little fiscal control or autonomy for local government as a result (Gray and Barford, 2018). In 2018, the National Audit Office reported that nationally there had been a 49.1% reduction of funding in real terms for local authorities between 2010–11 and 2017–18 and concluded that 'the government has announced multiple short-term funding initiatives in recent years and does not have a long-term funding plan for local authorities' (NAO, 2018: 10).

Lowndes and Gardner (2016) have argued that we are in an age of 'super-austerity', where new cuts for local government have come on top of previous ones, and while funding continues to tighten, demand for services – particularly social care and services associated with an ageing population – and the transference of risks from central government increase so that there is a risk to the ability of authorities to provide statutory services (NAO, 2018). This super-austerity, characterised by sustained and widespread cuts to funding and budgets, has defined much of Britain's public policy over the past decade and has prompted substantial restructuring in local government (Gray and Barford, 2018). Local government has become both a site and a target for fiscal retrenchment, charged with administering unprecedented budget cuts while also trying to provide local welfare programmes and catalyse local growth (Penny, 2017).

At the same time as the crisis of austerity, there is also commonly perceived to be a housing crisis in England, with rising property prices, declining affordability, falling rates of homeownership and rising levels of homelessness and housing inequality (Gallent et al, 2018). This crisis is widely reported in the media and in political and policy circles, with former Prime Minister Theresa May delivering a keynote speech in March 2018 about the 'national housing crisis' – meaning that 'in much of the country, housing is so unaffordable that millions of people who would reasonably expect to buy their own home are unable to do so. Others are struggling even to find somewhere to rent' (May, 2018) – and renaming the central government Department for Communities and Local Government as the Ministry of Housing, Communities and Local Government.

Housing is clearly vitally important. It is widely agreed that there is a human right to adequate housing, as set out in the 1948 United Nations Universal Declaration of Human Rights, which is seen as 'the basis of stability and security for an individual or family. The centre of our social, emotional and sometimes economic lives, a home should be a sanctuary; a place to live in peace, security and dignity' (UN Rapporteur for the Right to Housing, 2017, in Hearne, 2017: 62). As T'Hart and Boin (2001) note, however, while some crises clearly impose themselves inescapably (things like natural disasters), events are rather more ambiguous in many other crises and the very naming of certain social conditions or clusters of events as a 'crisis' is itself a political feat. Similarly, Hay (1996) notes the way power resides in the ability not only to respond to crises, but also to identify and define a crisis in the first place: 'Crises, then, are constituted in and through narrative. Such narratives must recruit the contradictions and failures of the system as "symptom"-atic of a more general condition of crisis ... [and] as in need of decisive intervention' (Hay, 1996: 254). Once a crisis is constituted, it then provides political actors with a reform opportunity, a chance to punctuate routine policy making (T'Hart and Boin, 2001).

The housing 'crisis' in England can clearly be understood through this perspective. While there certainly are issues related to rising property prices, declining affordability, homelessness and general housing inequality, the causes are complex and longstanding. Theresa May's March 2018 speech as Prime Minister, however, presented a simplified view that 'the root cause of the crisis is simple. For decades this country has failed to build enough of the right homes in the right places' (May, 2018). This reflects a now well-established construction of the housing crisis as primarily a supply problem, which then legitimates a view of 'a market held back by over-zealous bureaucracy', which then in turn supports calls to reduce planning control (a key local government function) (Gallent et al, 2018) rather than considering potentially more fundamental issues that have created the crisis, including the decline in the provision of housing directly by the local state.

As Gallent et al (2018) argue, the housing crisis may not be a crisis (implying being sudden and containable), but rather structural and not about to reach a climax and resolution. For local authorities at the receiving end of severe budget cuts, however, the crisis of austerity will feel very much a crisis. This super-austerity was not actually inevitable but rather reflects a deliberate targeting by the coalition and Conservative governments (2010–20) of local government as a primary area for spending cuts (Grimshaw, 2013). Such 'self-imposed austerity' by the central state (Penny, 2017) has seen the fiscal crisis 'dumped' onto the local state (Gray and Barford, 2018).

We can, then, perhaps agree that there are crises of austerity and housing closely involving local government and, as we will see throughout this book, interrelated to each other, but also note the political and constructed nature of our understanding of these crises, which must be critically interrogated. In the remainder of this chapter, we consider in a little more depth the nature of the crisis of local government austerity and the housing crisis, as well as introducing some key conceptual ideas that potentially help understand the responses of the local state to them.

The crisis of super-austerity

The first crisis, then, is linked to the government's imposition of austerity onto the local state in England in 2010 and the resultant budget cuts. A recent report co-authored by the Local Government Information Unit and the *Municipal Journal* starts: 'the state of local government finances is dire ... the local government funding system is in desperate need of overhaul' (LGiU and *MJ*, 2020: 4) while Christophers (2019) notes that one financial crisis – that of the banking and financial sector – has now become another: that of local councils.

The degree to which this crisis was necessary is, however, debated. First, there is the question of whether public sector budget cuts were needed or indeed advisable following the financial crash in 2008, with Gamble (2015) arguing that national debt in 2010 was not particularly high (seen in historic context) and could have been managed without such severe cuts to public expenditure had not the Treasury reverted to its standard approach to a fiscal crisis of retrenchment to try to maintain credibility with the markets. Similarly, Bailey et al (2015) note that while there was declining tax income and rising demand for public services following the sharp 6% drop in Gross Domestic Product (GDP) from 2008 to 2009, and so concern with government borrowing and credit ratings, these economic and fiscal problems did not need to automatically have led to the austerity solution adopted, which must be seen as a political choice. In other words, austerity was not an inevitable response to the sovereign debt crisis (Lowndes and Gardner, 2016).

Beyond the general political choice to reduce public sector expenditure to a deep scale and at a rapid pace, a further political choice made by the UK coalition government of 2010–15, and continued by the subsequent Conservative governments, was about how to distribute these cuts across government departments and areas of expenditure. There was a political choice to focus these cuts on the funding given to local government by central government. Again, there is debate here, this time as to whether this was a deliberate or a more accidental act of statecraft. For the latter, some have suggested that the particularly harsh treatment of local government was an accidental by-product of trying to preserve funding to other services, like health (Bailey et al, 2015). It is also notable that municipalities in other parts of the world are also having to manage austerity, for example with Dutch municipalities facing a similar pattern of cutbacks, retrenchment and downsizing (Overmans and Noordegraaf, 2014).

There are, however, other suggestions that there was a view that local government might be able to absorb cuts of this scale better than other public service institutions (due to a history of adaptation) (Travers, 2012, in Fitzgerald and Lupton, 2015) or that this was an intentional attempt to try to reshape local government, driving greater fiscal autonomy (Bailey et al, 2015) or a restructuring of the state (Lowndes and Gardner, 2016). Crewe (2016: 6) argues that the Conservatives had been wanting to transform local government ever since the 1980s, felt that it had lived for years on 'unsustainable growth and public finance' and so needed to be targeted. Lowndes and Gardner (2016), meanwhile, argue that the combination of devolution deals and austerity cuts show an attempt to shift responsibility and blame for cuts and resultant service reductions and that the accompanying rhetoric that cuts could be absorbed through 'smarter state' policies were little more than a tired recycling of New Public Management diktats.

Whatever the politics and internationalities, the scale of the cuts was dramatic. The-then Department for Communities and Local Government (DCLG) took the largest cut of any government department under the coalition government (Lowndes and Gardner, 2016), with most of this passed on to central government at a pace faster than that in most other developed countries (Bailey et al, 2015). The Comprehensive Spending Review of October 2010 proposed a 27% cut in central government funding for local government, alongside cuts to other funding streams that also impact local communities, with £81 billion of savings outlined up to 2014/15 and then a further £10 billion of cuts up to 2018 being announced in 2012 (Lowndes and McCaughie, 2013; Clayton et al, 2016).

Various figures are given by different sources for the scale of cuts that did then follow the 2010 announcements, all huge. The National Audit Office has reported that from the 2010/11 financial year to 2015/16, local authorities had experienced a real-term decline in government funding of 36%, with a further 5.7% reduction then predicted up to 2019/20 (NAO, 2017a). The result was a 28.6% reduction in local authority spending power from 2010/11 to 2017/18 (NAO, 2018), although note that Crewe (2016) suggests it was a 37% reduction in spending from 2010 to 2016: from 5.1% to 3.6% of GDP (Fitzgerald and Lupton, 2015). At the same time, over the first few years of these cuts, locally raised income also fell, not offsetting reductions in central government, with the requirement for a local referendum to increase council tax above centrally prescribed levels (NAO, 2014).

The cuts have been unprecedented in scale, representing the most significant reorganisation of public spending since the Second World War (Taylor-Goody, 2012, in Lowndes and Gardner, 2016). The cuts are more than three times those experienced during the 1978–85 period of austerity for English local government (Penny, 2017). This age of austerity (called 'savage austerity' by Christophers, 2019) has led to an existential threat to many local authorities, with Northamptonshire County Council effectively going bankrupt in February 2018 and West Somerset Council being merged into Taunton Deane Council in 2019 because it was no longer financially viable as a freestanding local authority.

The cuts have been particularly impactful because local government in the UK has been characterised for decades by its highly centralised funding. As local government is not included within a written constitution, as in most other countries, its powers are defined and limited by individual pieces of central legislation. Local government has no powers to raise taxation and is limited to raising money through small-scale fees and charges, some of which are also controlled by central government, such as fees for planning applications. Comparatively little is funded by locally raised council tax, which is calculated on the basis of property values as they stood in 1993, with little differential between the lowest and highest rates. These levels have not been uprated since, due to political cowardice on the part of central government (Crewe, 2016). Business rates have traditionally been locally raised but then redistributed by central government. Local money from the sale of assets, income from investments, external trading fees and charges and transfers from accumulated reserves can also provide some income (nationally this was 17% of income in 2013 (Fitzgerald and Lupton, 2015).

More significant has been the RSG from central to local government. In 2009–10, local authorities across England received between 36% and 82% of their income from this grant, allocated by central government mechanisms that were based on a principle of the redistribution of tax revenue to areas with the highest need (Gray and Barford, 2018). The grant has antecedents that go back a long way: central government grant funding of local government in England stretches back to the 19th century, with the idea of 'funding following duties'. There were consequently large increases after the Second World War on the basis that local government would deliver more welfare state services and that there was a shared national interest in such provision (Sandford, 2016). The RSG was on a reduced taper from 2013 and was cut completely by 2020. But, Britain has for decades arguably been the most centralised country in the developed world, with 91% of all funds raised in taxation controlled and allocated by central government, which is then able to exert considerable power over the funding and spending of local government (Crewe, 2016).

Beyond the general pattern of dependence on central government grants (and so vulnerability to cuts in this), there is, however, a geography to this austerity. It is urban areas – metropolitan districts and London boroughs, in particular – that were most reliant on the RSG, with high need from significant concentrations of poverty and deprivation, and so will face the largest fall in government funding (Lowndes and McCaughie, 2013; NAO, 2014; Bailey et al, 2015; Hastings et al, 2017). This reveals a structural unfairness in this crisis of local austerity as the poorer an area, the more reliant it has been on central government grants and the less likely it will be to benefit from government policies like the local retention of business rates and the New Homes Bonus, which favour those areas that already have stronger local economies and higher-value housing (Crewe, 2016). These poorest places now suffer most from diminished public services, less basic infrastructure and are locations where an electoral revenge is being seen (Gray and Barford, 2018; Rodriguez-Pose, 2018).

Beyond this pattern, micro-geographies can also see some authorities having a higher proportion of high-valued properties and so a bigger council tax base (Fitzgerald and Lupton, 2015). Further, some authorities in more affluent areas have had a historically low council tax base and minimal reserves and have now come under immense financial pressure – for example, Northamptonshire, the Isle of Wight and West Somerset. Overall, there is a move away from the principle of spatial redistribution and equalisation, which has been in place in relation to local government funding in some way since the late 19th country (Penny, 2017).

There is also a political dimension to the redistribution model used by central government where additional factors add weighting to those areas that are electorally in support of the party in government at the time. This generally represents a swing between urban and rural areas when national governments change hands. However, the result of the 2019 general election, where the Conservative Party won a large number of parliamentary seats in the former Labour northern heartlands, sometimes called the 'Red Wall', poses new challenges for a government that traditionally supports its more rural, southern electorate as it has to address the needs of northern areas that have been voiceless and lower-funded for a decade (Cutts et al, 2020; McCurdy et al, 2020). This can be considered to fit a wider trend of the 'electoral revenge' of left-behind places (Rodriguez-Pose, 2018).

As well as a geographical dimension, the cuts have also tended to follow a differentiation by service area. For those local authorities responsible for adult social care, this has become a pressing demand, accounting for 39% of all non-schools expenditure in 2015/16 (NAO, 2017a) and being cut by just 3% from 2010/11 to 2016/17 (NAO, 2018) – as opposed to a 46% reduction in real terms in spending on planning and development services (NAO, 2014). The increasing demand for adult social care has, in particular, driven the increasing cost pressures for local authorities and it is the combination of this and the decreasing central government funding that led local authorities like Birmingham and Newcastle to produce the so-called 'jaws of doom' graph (Figure 1.1), illustrating the very challenging combination of drastic cuts and increasing demand – a 'perfect storm' (Lowndes and McCaughie, 2013: 546).

Figure 1.1: Birmingham City Council's 'jaws of doom' budget projection from a 2012 consultation document

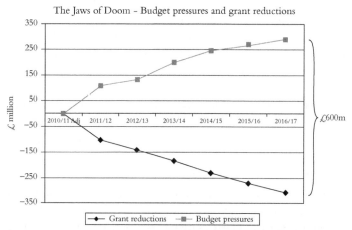

Source: Inlogov (2013); reproduced with permission of Birmingham City Council

The consequences of this central government-imposed austerity have been varied but following similar patterns across multiple authorities. Unsurprisingly, local authorities' spending decisions are influenced by the size of the fall in their spending power and some authorities are apparently showing persistent signs of financial stress (NAO, 2014). Gamble comments that 'central government was able to offload responsibility for the cuts on to local councils, a familiar story from British fiscal politics, reflecting the highly centralised nature of British government' (Gamble, 2015: 54). Lowndes and Gardner (2016) are concerned that the cuts might have multiplier effects and that the Cameron government's response that authorities just needed to do more for less through back-office efficiencies ignored the substantial savings that had already been made by local government over many years. In a recent survey, 74% of English local councils reported not feeling confident in the sustainability of local government finance, with 77% lacking confidence in the government's proposal that they can in future retain 100% of the business rates they raise locally as a way to fund local authorities (LGiU and *MJ*, 2020). Moor and Sandford (2017) explain this new business rate retention scheme, while Sandford (2017) argues that it is actually seeing some continued notion of equalisation between authorities able to raise higher rates through more economic prosperity and those that cannot, than had been originally appreciated. Nevertheless, the overall pattern of local government funding is much changed from ten years ago. Local authorities are receiving far less from central government, with some of the biggest cuts in areas of highest need for services.

Unable to simply meet the cuts through the 'mystical' powers of increased efficiencies, authorities have instead tended to make widespread spending cuts, seeing reductions in capital expenditure, particularly as they have not been able to support the costs of serving borrowing from their revenue budgets (NAO, 2016), and major job losses (Ward et al, 2015). Making cuts to services is not straightforward, including those services that are outsourced and where contract payments are fixed, taking an increasing amount of a dwindling budget (NAO, 2016). The web of obligations that fall on local authorities is what Overmans and Noordegraaf (2014) refer to as the 'constraints of publicness', but these obligations fall into statutory and discretionary duties, which authorities have provided for a variety of reasons. While it is these so-called 'discretionary' services that have seen the sharpest cuts, with only 36% of authorities apparently able to comfortably provide any non-statutory duties in 2020/21 (NAO, 2018; LGiU and *MJ*, 2020), authorities have a legal duty to promote the wellbeing of their areas as set out in the Local Government Act 2000. This effectively makes all duties statutory if they are needed. In relation to duties, that includes specific legally defined service requirements, which have also seen some cuts, with authorities concerned about the risk of costly judicial reviews in relation to their service provision and 12% of authorities apparently concerned they will not even be able to provide even core statutory services properly this year (NAO, 2018; LGiU and *MJ*, 2020). Children's services and education are seen as the top immediate pressures for councils nationally, followed by adult social care, housing and homelessness (LGiU and *MJ*, 2020).

Looking across services, the National Audit Office reported in 2014 that:

> Local authorities have tried to protect statutory services … spending on adult and children's social care has been relatively protected. Environmental and regulatory services, which include statutory duties to collect and dispose of waste, have also seen lower spending reductions than other areas. Areas with a higher proportion of spending on discretionary activities, such as planning and development, and housing, have seen much larger reductions. (NAO, 2014: 8)

There have been examples of services being cut completely, with closures of youth centres and day centres, and cutbacks to parks, allotments, libraries and leisure centres (Fitzgerald and Lupton, 2015). Adult social care is seen as the key long-term financial pressure for authorities, and there has arguably been a great 'risk shift' from central to local government around social protection (Bailey et al, 2015).

To try to continue to provide services, authorities have often drawn down on their reserves, with 57% reporting that they will do this in 2020 (LGiU and *MJ*, 2020). For a variety of historical and institutional factors, however, the level of reserves varies between authorities, with some having much weaker financial resilience, which can then increase inequality between different councils and any notion of territorial/spatial justice (Gray and Barford, 2018; NAO, 2018). With reductions in the range, reach and quality of public services and a smaller local employment base being provided by local authorities directly (Hastings et al, 2017), it has been argued that England 'has in the last six years become a darker, dirtier and more dangerous place' (Crewe, 2016: 4) and that 'there are hundreds of local examples of the impact of austerity, each unhappy in its own way, but it is only when they are viewed in aggregate that a picture emerges of an entire social infrastructure being destroyed' (Crewe, 2016: 3).

Alongside drawing down on reserves, authorities have also tried to raise funds through other means. As already mentioned, council tax is insufficient to fund services alone, but as part of the drive to raise more funds, 97% of councils planned to increase this in 2020/21. Alongside this, through business rate retention schemes and initiatives such as the New Homes Bonus (paid by central government to local government based on the delivery of new housing units, primarily by the private sector, in their areas), authorities have increasingly been incentivised to promote 'local growth', which in effect is the designated release of more land for private sector housing development rather than an integrated local economic growth plan. This has created some financial opportunities but also increased risks and uncertainty (NAO, 2014, 2020) as service provision becomes increasingly financially dependent on local economic development (Pugalis and McGuiness, 2013, in Penny, 2017) and commercial property investment income. As Bailey et al (2015) argue, an unsuccessful strategy may lead to lower growth, higher needs and so a reduced ability to provide services. Authorities have also been selling assets, especially land and property and trying to increase their own income from commercial sources such as sales, fees and charges, which increased 31% from 2013–14 to 2016–17 (Christophers, 2019). There has also been innovation to try to look for new sources of income (Hastings et al, 2017; NAO, 2018). Such innovation has included the use of authorities' ability to establish companies, particularly in relation to commercial property investment and housing development, which we focus on throughout this book.

For now, though, it is sufficient to note that centrally imposed austerity has created a crisis for local government in England and we have moved into a new era (Pollitt, 2010, in Overmans and Noordegraaf, 2014). This economic statecraft represents an ideological vision, which can be understood as wanting to radically reduce what is perceived as an oversized public sector, a 'right-wing assault on the welfare state, the collective provision of public services' (Grimshaw, 2013: 581). This has understandably been linked to the longer neoliberal project to reshape and redefine the state, with Peck (2012, in Hastings et al, 2017) arguing that contemporary neoliberal austerity (seen in many nations) operates downwards in both social and scalar terms, offloading on cities and communities and concentrating costs and burdens on those at the bottom of the social hierarchy (Peck, 2012, in Hastings et al, 2017). This has also potentially changed the power relationships between central and local government, which we return to in Chapter Five.

Some commentators have called this 'austerity urbanism' (for example, Watt and Minton, 2016), noting that the cuts and challenges have been concentrated in cities; however, there are examples of rural authorities across England that have also faced severe budget cuts, and so we prefer the concept of 'austerity localism' (Featherstone et al, 2012, in Clayton et al, 2016). In the face of such austerity localism, it is easy to be pessimistic. The crisis is severe, and consequences all too real. Crewe (2016: 1) has argued that 'the creation of the British state was a municipal project, and the state is now being unmade by the collapse of that project'; but, without diminishing the challenges, there have also been new opportunities and possibilities for local government in this increasingly risky and uncertain environment (Bailey et al, 2015). We will explore some of these opportunities and possibilities in this book, but first it is important to consider the other great contemporary crisis closely involving the local state: the housing crisis.

The housing crisis

The second local authority crisis revolves around that most fundamental human need: the need for shelter. As we explore in Chapter Two, local government in England has a long history of providing housing directly itself. It also has an important role, through planning, for facilitating new housing development by other parties. The housing crisis, then, is intimately linked to the local state. The crisis is, however, as already alluded to, more complex than has often been presented.

The crisis must be situated within the context of the nature of the UK housing system, which includes a fiscal system favouring owner-occupation (particularly due to the gains accruing from house price rises), a highly deregulated finance market but with a small number of large mortgage providers, inadequate supply and volatility in house prices and market activity associated with changes in demand arising from variations in economic growth and expectations (Whitehead and Williams, 2011). Some of these issues are seen in other housing markets internationally, but not all and there are particularities that are important to understanding the various issues.

The National Audit Office reported in 2017 on the English housing stock, which in 2015 comprised 23.5 million homes (NAO, 2017c). Of these, 62% were owner-occupied, 20% were privately rented and 17% were socially rented. Of the home, 20% were 'non-decent' in terms of an official definition of housing quality (NAO, 2017c). The housing stock was estimated to have a total value of £5.6 trillion in 2015, an increase of £1 trillion since 2010 (NAO, 2017c).

The public sector spent £28 billion on housing in 2015–16, including £1.15 billion spent by local authorities on homelessness services during 2015–16, a rise of 22% in real terms since 2010–11 (NAO, 2017a, 2017c). Tackling homelessness is a statutory responsibility of local authorities, and the rising number of homeless people is a key component of any definition of the housing crisis. The ending of private sector tenancies has overtaken all other causes to become the biggest driver of statutory homelessness in England, representing 32% of households accepted as homeless by local authorities in 2016–17 (NAO, 2017b). There were 77,240 households in temporary accommodation in England in 2017, an increase of 60% from 2011, and this included 120,540 children (NAO, 2017b). Temporary accommodation accounts for more than three quarters of public spending on homelessness (NAO, 2017b).

The issues of homelessness are closely related to the issues of affordability, which have sometimes been overlooked by a focus on the overall number of new housing units delivered. Problems of worsening affordability (Whitehead and Williams, 2011) have been linked to the fact that, over recent decades, there has been an increase in homeownership and the number of privately rented homes, but a reduction in social rented homes. Social housing rents have increased faster than earnings since 2001–02, while housing has become less affordable for first-time buyers as well (NAO, 2017c). Until 1980, local authorities were primary providers of social housing, funded by central government grant funding. This housing was partly delivered by local authorities and partly by the private construction sector, but all the resulting dwellings were managed by local authorities. In 1979, Margaret Thatcher committed to introduce tenants' right to buy their home in the Conservative Party election manifesto (Shipman, 2015). There have been waves of Right to Buy (RTB) initiatives since this approach was implemented in 1980, frequently accompanied by promises of funding to replace the number of social housing units lost to the public sector through these sales (Murie, 2016). This provision has never occurred and the continuing rules surrounding the reuse of RTB receipts has made it very difficult for councils to provide replacement housing in a viable way. Our own research has found that only 65% of councils were using their RTB receipts in 2018, with the rest returning this funding to government via Homes England because the rules made it difficult to spend the funds within the short time limit and in the specific ways required. In London, current Mayor Sadiq Khan received these funds rather than Homes England and in 2018 he devised a 'bank' system where unused RTB receipts that were returned to him were specifically kept for later use by each borough. RTB continues to present a stark challenge in the provision of sufficient genuinely affordable housing.

A social housing green paper, *A new deal for social housing*, published in August 2018, sought to recognise the role of social housing and the need for more prioritisation on social and affordable housing provision than there has been in the recent past (MHCLG, 2018c). Changes in the role of housing associations, to become more mainstream developers, like the private sector, have also reduced the amount of social and affordable housing provision each year. For both local authorities and housing associations, this has also been related to the reduction in housing subsidies that have been available from the government and a switch in government policy from 2012 onwards to assume that social and affordable housing would be a residual function of the private housing market. By giving developers support for sales-for-market housing through the interim sales loans for short-term discounts and Help to Buy schemes, the government has primarily been using subsidy to support developers that provide about 50% of the total housing provision each year. However, other types of need have not been directly funded to the same level, which is estimated to be between £22 billion and £32 billion from 2015 to 2022 (Morphet and Clifford, 2019).

It is perhaps unsurprising, then, that housing has become one of the government's key priorities. The tendency has been, however, to focus mostly on the overall number of homes being built in England, rather than other factors linked to the crisis: debate has increasingly been about questions of supply (Gallent et al, 2018). These supply-side issues are discussed in the 2017 housing White Paper (MHCLG, 2017) and there has been an overall government target to see the delivery of one million new homes across England from 2015 to 2020 (NAO, 2017c), but with an emphasis on the role of private sector housebuilders in delivering this. However, in their 2019 review of housing provision, the National Audit Office could not find any evidential basis for this target figure of new homes. A longer review of government housing policies is provided in Morphet and Clifford (2017, 2019).

The biggest contributor of new housing in England since the Thatcher period has been private sector housebuilders, who have increased their output over this period, although with noticeable variation according to economic and market conditions and a decline in smaller builders since the 2008 financial crash with the dominance of a small number of major housebuilding groupings (Morphet and Clifford, 2017). Indeed, the financial crash has rapid impacts on the supply of new housing by the private market (Whitehead and Williams, 2011).

The undersupply of new housing predates the financial crash, however. As the National Audit Office reported in 2017:

> Housebuilding in England has not kept pace with need, particularly in London. Since the 1980s, demand for housing in England has increased. Housebuilding, however, has not kept pace with demand. Public sector housebuilding has fallen and the number of homes added by the private sector has been vulnerable to both economic recessions and the cost of finance to potential homeowners. Between 2001 and 2010, an average of 144,000 new homes were completed annually: 100,000 fewer per year than in the 1970s. (NAO, 2017c: 6)

In response to this undersupply, politicians and think tanks from the right have tended to blame restrictions from the planning system and call for liberalisation of the system (Gallent et al, 2017). One form of deregulation of planning regulations – permitted development for the conversion of commercial buildings (like offices) to residential use in England – has, however, produced noticeably poor-quality housing (Clifford et al, 2019).

Interestingly, however, the focus on the supply side of the housing debate has also been a focus for the left, who have tended to highlight the decline of, and need for, more public sector building (Gallent et al, 2017). As we discuss further in Chapter Two, local authorities provided a significant share of new housing in the 20th century, for example from 1946 to 1961, 90% of London's new housing was provided by local authorities (Watt and Minton, 2016) and 1.5 million new homes were completed by local authorities from 1950 to 1959 (Morphet and Clifford, 2017). This changed through policies like RTB, with social rent dropping from being 32% of households in England in 1981 to 18% by 2008 (Whitehead and Williams, 2011). Only 8,000 new council homes were delivered from 2010 to 2015 (Morphet and Clifford, 2017), with just 340 in the whole of London from 1997/98 to 2009/10 (Watt and Minton). There has been a shift of attention in the recent past from local authorities providing social housing to housing associations providing this, the latter completing 150,000 homes from 2010 to 2015 (Morphet and Clifford, 2017), but this is still significantly below demand.

Central government grants for social housing have been almost completely withdrawn and, through the mantra of 'viability', the planning gains from private sector developers funding social housing (the key route to delivering affordable housing over recent years being such residual contributions from private market development) have been diminishing (Beswick and Penny, 2018). Graphs such as Figure 1.2 are widely circulated and those on the left will often suggest a return to council housebuilding as a route to resolving the housing crisis, potentially tackling issues of both the overall number of units being built but also their affordability.

Figure 1.2: Provision of new housing units in England through the post-war period

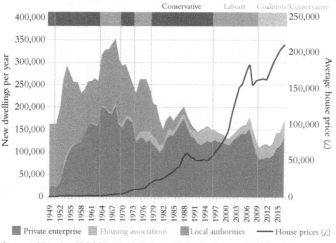

Source: Murphy (2018); reproduced with permission of IPPR

Such supply-side considerations clearly do matter: the collapse in public social housing provision, the restrictions that are inevitably associated with planning regulation (albeit with other benefits from such regulation), construction industry inefficiencies and public policy do play a big role in our housing crisis (Ryan-Collins, 2019). However, in discussing the housing crisis, it is important to note that they do not represent the whole picture. A policy debate that has almost exclusively focused on supply-side dynamics has neglected important considerations on the demand side. That this is a necessary consideration can be seen by the fact that planning controls have existed since the late 1940s, and that countries such as Spain and Ireland with much more liberal systems than England also experienced housing affordability problems in the run-up to the financial crash despite delivery exceeding need in terms of new household formation numbers (Aalbers and Hailia, 2018; Ryan-Collins, 2019).

Considering the demand side shifts attention to the supply of money directed towards housing. Gallent et al (2018) argue that the changing role of the state in the production of housing was one key issue that led to the housing crisis, but the other was the change in desired function of housing from shelter to being an investment and savings vehicle – a wealth machine – in England. Looking at the demand side involves considering not just the demographic changes – such as an ageing population and more single households – that drive housing demand (with issues in terms of a lack of private sector housing delivery for an ageing population), but also the way that investment in housing as an asset drives the housing crisis.

Housing has become central to the contemporary capitalist political economy, with Aalbers (2016, in Aalbers and Hailia, 2018) arguing that a global wall of money is looking for high-quality collateral investments and housing is one of the few such assets, with rising and secure property values seen as driving investors who then further increase house prices (see also Beswick et al, 2016). Ryan-Collins (2019) argues that the housing affordability and wealth inequality crises in many developed nations are created by a feedback cycle between finance and landed property, linked to the increasing policy preference for private homeownership and the liberalisation of bank credit, which he terms a 'housing-finance cycle'. Thus, 'housing and real estate ... have become a privileged element of the financial strategies of households' (Coq-Huelva, 2013: 1218).

As higher house prices primarily create housing wealth for those who already own a house (including landlords), the demand for housing for wealth generation – with house price rises seen by many successive UK governments as a form of good inflation – drives the housing crisis, and the concentration of investment capital makes the housing market dysfunctional (Gallent, 2016). It is unsurprising that in this context there has been a rapid expansion of amateur landlordism in England, fuelled by buy-to-let mortgages and furthering the view of housing as a market commodity rather than a social good (Gallent et al, 2017). A more welfarist view of the role and provision of housing persists in the policies and programmes of the UK devolved administrations in Scotland, Wales and Northern Ireland.

Given that the majority of mortgage loans finance the purchase of existing rather than new property, and the supply of bank mortgage credit creates its own increased demand, Ryan-Collins (2019: 7) argues that the housing crisis will not be solved through increased supply: 'however fast you can build, banks can create new credit faster'. Instead, regulatory and structural changes to banks, so that business lending is preferred over property lending, are needed to break the crisis (see also Gallent et al, 2018). Such demand-side reform is largely beyond the control of the local state and is not the focus of this book. However, it is useful to consider a fuller understanding of the components of the housing crisis by way of context for what is going on in relation to local authorities, property and housing. Furthermore, the debate over housing as a social good versus housing as an investment vehicle is very relevant to the recent activity of local authorities around the direct delivery of housing, as we explore in the following chapters.

The housing crisis is an issue of national significance, and considerable policy debate surrounds it. There are pressing issues of homelessness and a lack of affordable housing, which concern local government and directly relate to its statutory duties. In terms of the supply of housing, there has been a concentration by central government over recent years on planning reform to allow the market to deliver more housing (further discussed in Chapter Two), with planning an important statutory function of local government in England. There has also been an increasing question about the role of local government in relation to a return to its historic role of directly delivering housing in relation to issues of affordability. The local state is centrally involved in the housing crisis, and this has driven activity that we explore through the rest of this book.

Financialisation and municipal entrepreneurialism

In exploring the role of local government in the direct delivery of housing, and the use of property and housing as investment vehicles to try to tackle austerity, our work is situated within broader academic debate surrounding the key concepts of 'financialisation' and 'municipal entrepreneurialism'. Financialisation has been defined by Aalbers (2017: 544) as 'the increasing dominance of financial actors, markets, practices, measurements and narratives, at various scales, resulting in a structural transformation of economies, firms (including financial institutions), states and households'. It has become a 'shorthand for the increasing influence of financial actors, relations, logics and practices in the economy on firms, states, people and places' (Pike et al, 2019: 45) and reflects the shift in the focus of economic activity from production to finance (Forrest, 2015). It is argued that financialisation provides a new governance mode, under which state strategies are increasingly realised through financially mediated means and in conjunction with credit market actors and intermediaries (Peck and Whiteside, 2016, in Loon et al, 2019).

The concept of financialisation has been closely linked with housing. Ryan-Collins (2019), for example, has described housing as a key channel to maintain demand in the face of stagnating wages and productively in late-modern capitalism, while Aalbers (2015) discusses the transformation of global capitalism under financialisation as closely linked with local and national housing markets. Flows of credit, unprecedented levels of debt using housing as a form of collateral and resulting inflated housing prices leads to an increasing entwinement of financial markets and the built environment (Guironnet et al, 2016; Watt and Minton, 2016; Aalbers, 2017). In other words, investment demand and the use of housing as collateral for money and wealth creation under a housing-dependent banking system in the UK can be understood as a process of 'financialisation' and helps to explain the housing crisis (Gallent et al, 2017). The intensification of housing being a financial commodity, valued for exchange rather than use value, has arguably worsened inequality (Fainstein, 2016).

The concept of financialisation has also been applied to understanding transformations in the funding of the local state. Much of this work has explored the way that austerity hit local governments in the United States and how they have used markets to further their own agendas. An example of this is Weber's (2010) account of the way Chicago devised the financial instrument of Tax Increment Financing to help fund the costs of urban redevelopment (in Guironnet et al, 2016). It is argued that municipalities increasingly rely on creative financial engineering, using assets as collateral and sources of revenue to support the provision of services (Gotham, 2016, in Beswick and Penny, 2018; Loon et al, 2019). This can apparently include a so-called financialisation of local infrastructure, which is explored by Pike et al (2019), who argue that the local state is both the object and agent of financialisation: 'through engagement with financial actors, local governments are simultaneously the focus of financialisation and its originator. This acceleration and "growing integration" between the municipal state and financial system is compelling local governments to behave more commercially like private businesses and transforming the ideologies, structures, practices and expressions of the state' (Pike et al, 2019: 56). Beswick and Penny (2018) argue that this process can also include local housing assets, so that there is a link between housing financialisation and the financialisation of the local state.

The concept of 'financialisation' has become a 'buzz word' or meta-narrative in the social sciences, often held to be one of the defining features of late-modern capitalism (alongside globalisation and neoliberalism; Christophers, 2015), but it has been debated. Christophers (2015) is concerned about the risk of overstating the scale of finance's significance as opposed to other factors in governance, the lack of conceptual clarity and precision around financialisation, and also claims to its historical novelty. He highlights the way that 19th-century urban slums were the product of the financial calculations of private developers (Shaw, 1892) and comments that '[o]nly from the mid-1930s to the mid-1970s, in the leading Western industrialized nations, was finance truly shackled' (Christophers, 2015: 193). Similarly, Ward (2017, in Beswick and Penny, 2018) has called for a more careful historicisation of the term and practices for which financialisation is summonsed to account. Aalbers (2017) responds to the concern about conceptual precision by noting that this is not unusual with many concepts used in the social sciences, with an underlying conceptualisation of financialisation as a rationale or logic of finance penetrating different, hitherto non-financial things.

The concept of financialisation has been used in relation to activities of local government in the UK relevant to this book. Christophers (2018) provides an account of how the UK state has treated its own land holdings, charting the tendency to sell public land to private actors, treating it a financial asset rather than considering its use value and thus acting as a facilitator of financialisation. This is a trend that we will argue has declined as land is instead actively used for housing delivery directly by local authorities. The establishment of a housing company by Lambeth Council is considered by Beswick and Penny (2018), who argue that the authority is actively executing financialisation by constituting its public housing estates as sites of extraction for financial capital. They see this as treating public land as a quasi-financial asset, with a new urban governance logic, which is aggressively commercial and speculative. Christophers (2019) also draws on the notion of financialisation when considering the scale of the establishment of local authority housing and property companies in England.

This book does not specifically seek to provide a detailed engagement with the concept of financialisation; however, we do consider the concept as part of the context for our work. We believe it is important to take account of the longer history of local government and the attempts to see housing delivered – more about the use value of land than just the exchange value – in relation to applying the concept to the activities of the local state in England in response to austerity and the housing crisis. We return to this in the concluding chapter of this book.

Notions of financialisation have been linked to the wider idea of a shift from post-war managerial logics of urban governance to a neoliberal entrepreneurial regime (Guironnet et al, 2016). In a seminal piece, David Harvey defined urban entrepreneurialism as resting on 'public-private partnership focusing on investment and economic development with the speculative construction of place rather than amelioration of conditions within a particular territory as its immediate (though by no means exclusive) political and economic goal' (Harvey, 1989, in Phelps and Miao, 2019: 2) and this work is commonly cited in work that periodises urban politics and associated bureaucratic focus and action with the view that traditional urban managerialism has been replaced by new forms of urban entrepreneurialism. It has been argued that, in the context of the global financial crisis and austerity, there is an increasing shift to urban entrepreneurialism (O'Brien et al, 2019) in the late neoliberal period (Aalbers, 2015).

Beswick and Penny (2018) consider the turn to more entrepreneurial solutions to deliver more housing, through special purpose vehicle housing companies, as 'financialised municipal entrepreneurialism'. Thompson et al (2020) argue that there has been a resurgence in municipalism – the relative power of municipalities over political and economic governance – with a desire to break with neoliberal austerity seen in many places. The response can, however, take divergent forms across 'an assemblage of competing adaptive and experimental strategies of governance in, against and beyond "late-entrepreneurial" urban political economy' (Thompson et al, 2020: 3). Indeed, Phelps and Miao (2019) attempt to consider the multitude of activities and approaches that have sometimes been labelled urban entrepreneurialism and suggest a typology of four varieties – new urban managerialism, urban diplomacy, urban intrapreneurialism and urban speculation – distinguished by differing economic logics, emphasis, content, scope and social implications.

A key strand of contemporary municipal entrepreneurialism in England has involved utilising assets in land to build new housing and buying commercial property to create alternative revenue streams. A recent survey shows that 86% of councils in England said that exploring other sources of income (beyond council tax and business rates) was a high priority or essential and 66% thought that councils would become more reliant on income from commercial investments in the future. Local housing and commercial developments are high on the list of preferred income-generating activities, with 75% of authorities reporting that they are exploring commercial developments, 71% are looking at housing developments and 47% are investing in energy projects this year (LGiU and *MJ*, 2020). It is argued that this is evidence of councils taking 'bold decisions to generate new income ... address the challenges of the future [and] ... secure their council's long-term financial sustainability' (LGiU and *MJ*, 2020: 5). Christophers (2019) notes that councils have borrowed widely and heavily, doubling from £5 billion in 2013/14 to £10 billion in 2017/18 as part of a drive to generate their income by investing in commercial property and housing delivery. This results from operating at the intersection of devolved austerity, reformed housing finance and monetary policy and the constraints and opportunities of circumstance.

Local authorities have, however, been investing in buying commercial property to generate income for some time. So this is not entirely new. More broadly, the emergence of new commercial ventures is also redolent of 19th-century civic traditions (Lowndes and Gardner, 2016). In the late 19th century, local authorities, often acting on their own initiative, established their own gas, water, electricity and tramway companies. Crewe (2016) links this to their role in pioneering slum clearance, building housing, parks, hospitals, museums and libraries, with the income of municipal enterprises used to further improvements in their area. Skelcher (2017) explains how Birmingham City Council acquired privately run gas, electricity, water and tramway businesses from the 1870s to the 1910s, with the hope of improving the health and mobility of residents but also to generate income: the profits were then invested in urban redevelopment and cultural facilities.

It was in the post-war period that central government nationalisations of council-owned utility companies deprived local authorities of much of their independent income and made them more dependent on central government. Many new responsibilities of the rapidly expanding welfare state were delegated to local authorities, with a link to central government grant funding (John, 2014). It is notable that in response to Crewe's extolling of the virtues of such an imagined pre-war municipal golden age, Malpass (2017, in Crewe, 2016) suggests that the freedom for local councils in the 19th century to innovate and develop services was matched by a freedom not to do so. Thus, some authorities, like Birmingham, did indeed clear slums and build new houses, but many others, like Bristol, did not.

Conclusions

Local government in England is intimately linked to the crises of super-austerity and of housing. The lack of affordable housing, issues around housing delivery and issues in terms of income to fund services are real challenges. This provides the context for the response from local authorities we have seen around becoming more directly engaged in housing delivery again, and establishing housing and property companies, which draw on older traditions of municipal entrepreneurship. There is a clear need to understand further what local authorities are doing, why, and the extent of activity. Drawing on data collected through two research projects (reported in Morphet and Clifford, 2017, 2019), we seek to do just that in this book.

In the next chapter, we explore the history of housing development and planning for housing by local authorities in the UK. Chapter Three then considers the pushback against austerity by local authority housing companies and other forms of provision to deal with homelessness, housing provision and income generation, outlining what has been done, how and why. Chapter Four provides examples of different types of local authority across England to illustrate the impact of shared experience and growing confidence in the direct delivery of housing as a means of re-establishing local government's community credibility. Chapter Five then concludes the book through a consideration of what this move by local authorities together with other forms of municipal entrepreneurialism to defeat austerity may mean in the longer term for central–local government relationships in England and for housing delivery and the implications of recent activity.

TWO

Local government, housing and planning in the UK: a history

Introduction

The role and history of local government in the UK are inextricably linked with housing provision and delivery in its administrative areas (Reeves, 2006; Chandler, 2010). The period since 1980 within which local government's housing role was lessened and almost removed, particularly in England, has been important in understanding how its position has been undermined and reduced as viewed by local political leaders as well as the community (Dunleavy, 1984; Cochrane, 1991). This change in the real and perceived level of strength of local government through the removal of the housing function was intentional and meant to reduce the centrality of local government's relationship to its community and its local spending power (Stoker, 1988; Kelly, 2007; Rhodes, 2018). As the proponent of this change, the-then Prime Minister Margaret Thatcher intended to undermine much of local government's core support from Labour voters (Jessop et al, 1988; Evans, 2018). Yet the history of local authority provision of housing demonstrates that it has always been a contractual relationship offered by government and its removal was also part of the government's obligations to meet international treaty obligations (Morphet, 2017). In this chapter, this contractual relationship is considered as are the ways in which housing formed the basis of local government's place in the local community (Wills, 2016).

Housing responsibilities have given local authorities legitimacy in central–local debates and negotiations (Rhodes, 2018). In working to restore their role as housing providers, local authorities are seeking to fundamentally renegotiate their position within the state. In this chapter, we consider the history of local government's involvement in housing provision. Much of this history is UK-wide; however, following devolution, there have been some notable differences in housing policy between the nations of the UK in recent years (McKee et al, 2016), and our focus for the remainder of this book is on England. In Scotland (McKee, 2010) and Wales (Smith, 2018), housing provision by local authorities has continued and RTB provisions have been removed. In Northern Ireland, the public provision of housing is through the Housing Executive (Paris and Frey, 2018).

How did local authorities become involved in providing housing?

The establishment of modern local government in the form it is generally understood today was in 1888 and its creation was a culmination of national concerns for the ways in which growing populations were to be governed and supported, not least in reaction to the growing UK economy, which was then the largest in the world (Chandler, 2013). As Joseph Chamberlain demonstrated in Birmingham, having a labour force that was healthy, literate and well housed was an important component of any local economy and the initiatives that he undertook in Birmingham – through land acquisition, redevelopment, housing and education provision – were important exemplars in the development of municipal entrepreneurialism (Marsh and Gordon, 1995; Orr and Vince, 2009). While local authorities were explicitly tasked by central government with responsibilities for public health, their activities in providing housing were left to local decision making. In urban areas, it was clear that the provision of decent homes for working-class people could not be left to the market and, as George Bernard Shaw's (1892) play *Widowers' Houses* demonstrates, the rent rolls of poor-quality housing were being used by the upper and middle classes to support their incomes. Rental income for the same type of house was greater in East London compared with West London. Speculators were also purchasing poor-quality homes as a means of gaining compensation when redevelopment schemes were proposed. In urban areas, much housing was provided by charities and philanthropic foundations (Malpass, 2000; Mullins et al, 2006), who through their development of metropolitan dwellings, provided accommodation, some places to hang washing externally rather than inside the dwelling, and play areas for children. These were all philanthropic contributions to support the urban labour market (White, 2016a). Most of these dwellings for working-class people were built in central urban areas.

The Boer War in 1899 demonstrated that many younger working-class men were physically unfit to fight, which came to be seen as caused by poor-quality housing (Gilbert, 1965). It was also the case that returning soldiers had few places to live and the government was concerned that the military covenant was not being kept – a recurring stimulus to the public provision of housing in 1919 and 1945 (White, 2016b). The government introduced a new model where it provided funding for local authorities to develop housing to meet this need (Young and Garside, 1982) – the beginning of the client and contractor relationship between central and local government. However, it became clear that this encouragement was not enough to ensure that adequate volumes and types of housing were built and there were government concerns that local authorities were unfit for this task. The government started to consider taking different approaches.

The Housing and Planning Act 1909 set some of the ground rules that were stimulated by the emergence of the Garden City movement (Howard, 1898, 1902). The Act outlawed unhealthy back-to-back housing development and encouraged local authorities to create housing estates inspired by the Garden City principles. It also set local authorities to tackle substandard housing. While this Act included the first mention of the term 'town planning', Booth and Huxley (2012) argue that it was essentially about housing, with the town planning dimension concerned with the setting of housing rather than a wider and comprehensive approach that was encompassed by the Garden City movement. The Act required the establishment of public health and housing committees by county councils and was a consolidation of existing legislation for working-class housing provision. It also eased borrowing for housing made available by the government from the Public Works Loan Commission, which, for the first time, included roads as part of housing development. Local authorities were also given powers over private landlords to inspect and ensure that their premises were in good condition. More controversially, county councils were obliged to appoint medical officers of health who could intervene if the district councils were not performing their responsibilities. Booth and Huxley (2012) argue that this started a hierarchical approach to government and delivery as a consequence. This also deflected potential criticism for non-delivery of housing away from central government to local government.

After the First World War, the Housing and Town Planning Act 1919 – more commonly known as the 'Addison Act' – was introduced. This established the methods through which councils could provide housing in more systematic ways and as a duty (Wilding, 1973; Boughton, 2018; White, 2018). In the later stages of the First World War, there was a recognition that on the return of the military, housing would be a significant issue. At the same time, the Tudor Walters Report (Walters, 1918) indicated that there was no expectation that private sector housebuilders could adequately provide for these needs, particularly in the first few years after the war. It was also agreed that if such provision was to be made, then it had to be by local authorities. The councils had also been making their case that funding would need to be provided entirely from central government and over and above the local contribution equivalent to a penny rate. While there had been initial opposition to this approach, the power of local authorities working together achieved this change in the government's position. In return for this funding, the Housing and Town Planning Act 1919 made it a duty for local authorities to consider the needs in their areas for working-class housing and, within a three-month period, to submit proposals to government about how these new powers were to be exercised. This was regarded as a major win for local authorities. It was also the introduction of a formal role for local authorities in the delivery of housing. This increased their size and budget but also made them popular within their electorate. It also focused the delivery of housing by local authorities on meeting public health standards and being of good design (Swenarton, 2018). It also enhanced the role of the central government department responsible for local government. Wilding (1973: 334) also notes that, at the time, local government became the default provider of working-class homes, which also reflected that 'new and higher standards helped make subsidies a permanent feature of housing policy'. Many local authorities engaged on the provision of new homes in Garden City-inspired layouts on greenfield sites on their existing built-up edges. People were proud to move into them and, in some cases, chose a council tenancy over house purchase (Forster, 2014).

A second approach was to encourage the metropolitan councils such as London, Birmingham and Manchester to start to build on a larger scale through peripheral cottage and 'out county' estates (Jennings, 1971; Garside, 1983; Olechnowicz,

1997). This was not to undermine the role of smaller local authorities, but the government was already taking a centralised view that a more dispersed and localised approach would not meet all national requirements. Further, in the 1930s, as finance became more restricted, local authorities focused on rehousing those from slum clearance schemes and this had effects on the wider role of council housing (Balchin, 1998). However, in the 1930s and later, the national economic decline led to local authorities developing housing as a mechanism to provide work. Councils were also able to buy land and historic houses more cheaply and the scale of death duties meant that many large landowners were forced to sell their houses and land to pay this tax (Strong et al, 1974; Raven et al, 2015).

Councils were also purchasing large farms during the agricultural slump as a means of saving them from development. These agricultural holdings were meant to provide continuing employment for those working on the land and many local authorities continue to maintain these holdings in their asset portfolios to the present day, although others have been sold (Shrubsole, 2018, 2019). In many rural areas, councils provided cottage homes in villages for those working on the land and to support the rural economy. There were also concerns about the type of housebuilding, particularly in relation to ribbon development and low-density sprawl, which led to increased support for managed development (Sheail, 1979; Healey et al, 1988). The role of local authorities in planning all types of housing development and the way in which this related to their wider infrastructure investment for sewers, water and energy also became a central concern (Wilson, 1991). Many local authorities became energy companies – owning the local gas works – and there were also pressures to increase the number of energy users to support the maintenance and expansion of energy provision at the local level. In 1947, when electricity was nationalised on a regional basis, for example, the greatest number of suppliers included were local authorities (Parker, 2009).

As the expectation of war grew in the 1930s, there were concerns about the location and distribution of the population and manufacturing as set out in the Government Commission report entitled the Report of the Royal Commission on the Distribution of the Industrial Population – the Barlow Report (Barlow, 1940). The proposal to distribute the locations of manufacturing plants away from the more densely built-up areas was implemented through factory development along arterial roads as well as through the private sector by companies such as Slough Estates (Allen, 1951; Scott, 2001). The Barlow Commission proposed the creation of specific locations for factories rather than in town centres where they had grown from local workshops. This was seen as a means both to support the economy and to disperse industrial locations as potential targets (Heim, 1983; Ward, 1990). Further, by relocating companies at the urban periphery or on arterial roads, this provided opportunities for new housing – both public and private – to support their developments (Scott and Walsh, 2004).

In the immediate post-war period, after 1945, there was a national shortage of housing (McCrone and Stephens, 2017), but this period saw a rapid expansion of local authorities' role in the provision of housing (Malpass, 2005) and the emergence of regulation of land use through the town and country planning regime. The government also acted directly in both the provision of housing and the creation of a different type of development approach through the instigation of a new town programme (Clapson, 1998; Aldridge, 2017). As Malpass (2005) demonstrates, the development of housing was not only a means through which to meet the military covenant – for returning soldiers – but the government also saw it as a means of absorbing these retuning soldiers into the construction industry. The government was of the view that this task could be most quickly fulfilled through local authority construction of housing but, in due course, this role of housebuilding would eventually be led by the private sector.

This provision of housing was an example of another contracted relationship between central and local government. Local authorities were incentivised to build and manage housing for social rent to meet a number of government obligations (Turner, 2014). These included, in addition to meeting the fulfilment of the military covenant, replacing those homes that had been lost through bomb damage, addressing public health concerns through improving living conditions and stimulating the economy through capital investment. While all were government policies, it was local government that was regarded as the main provider of housing by local communities rather than there being much recognition that local authorities were central government's delivery arm. As the mechanisms for housing provision became more developed within local authorities, through the creation of architects' departments and direct labour organisations, these also became the target for the interest of the private sector-owned construction-related industries. As the government had intended, from the early 1940s, this private sector involvement in public sector housing delivery was initially through the provision of labour and then increasingly through construction and design contracts. The demand for building trades also supported the in-migration of workers, particularly from Ireland and the West Indies (Bresnen et al, 1985; Forster, 2014). As the housing delivery programme gathered pace in the 1950s, there were concerns about whether there was enough labour to meet all housing development expectations. Construction companies started to promote the use of new building techniques such as system building, which included some off-site construction using concrete components. However, public confidence was shaken with this method of construction when, in 1968, a new block, Ronan Point, collapsed two months after it had opened. This had a major effect on the use of system building (Pearson and Delatte, 2005), which is still remembered (Hazelton, 2019).

The role of housing development was important in the provision for post-war community cohesion and rebuilding society. There were expectations that council housing would be a preferred tenure for most people as very few could afford to purchase a home (Stevenson, 1991; Swenarton, 2018). Yet there were also issues emerging about maintaining the differences between council and owner-occupied homes, as witnessed in Oxford through the building of the Cutteslowe Walls to separate the two (Collison, 1963). There are also parallels between this post-war period and the current time: many of the construction companies that were in business delivering council housing in the 1950s and 1960s, lobbying the government for a continuation of the housing budgets to be used by contractors, have now become housing development companies (Holt et al, 1995). Further, the concerns about the delivery of new homes keeping pace with demand and loss of labour post-Brexit is also hastening the current government's support for modern methods of construction to reduce the need for skilled labour required for housebuilding.

Local authorities: funding for housing

The government established a specific means of accounting for the provision of public housing in the 1930s through the construction of the Housing Revenue Account (HRA). The HRA is not a separate fund nor does it have any application in any other form of accounting procedures. It is rather a ring-fenced account within which the government requires local authorities that retain more than 200 social rented homes, funded through specific borrowing and grant subsidy regimes that it has provided, to account for rent income and expenditure. The main items of expenditure included in the account are management and maintenance costs, major repairs, loan charges and depreciation costs, and it is held in the local authority's general fund. The ways in which local authorities with an HRA can borrow for further social housing development are controlled tightly by government and this has been the mechanism by which governments since 1980 have restricted local authorities building social rented homes supported by housing subsidy. At the same time, those tenants renting homes provided through the mechanism offered by the HRA were offered the opportunity to exercise their right to buy their home from 1980 onwards. Tenants of these HRA homes had been able to pass on their tenancies through general succession principles but this right was changed in 2012. Local authorities that now hold fewer than 200 or no social rented homes funded through the HRA do not have to establish an HRA. If local authorities use other means to provide housing, including those for social rent, cross-subsidised through other housing, the tenants do not have the same rights to succession or the right to buy.

In 2007, the UK government agreed to adopt the International Financial Reporting Standard (IFRS) for public sector accounting and this was to be introduced over a gradual period of time to conclude in 2017. The application of the IFRS in the public sector meant that private and public accounting reporting standards would be the same. The government, together with local government and other public bodies, worked to transition their accounting methods, producing twin accounts using both methods until 2017. These are now described as Whole Government Accounts, or Single National Accounts as they are known internationally, which are required as part of international trading agreements within the World Trade Organization (WTO). They identify the baseline national public expenditure against which the percentage open to competition will be measured (Morphet, forthcoming). The implication of the application of the IFRS is that the HRA should be abolished, as it is a political and not an accounting construct. Rather than any council's social housing assets being held in a circumscribed account, the effect of the IFRS would be to move them into the council's assets portfolio, which, like the private sector, they could use to secure debt for further investment. This is how all other countries within the Organisation for Economic Co-operation and Development (OECD) fund public housing investment. In the UK, HM Government decided that it would not implement this aspect of the IFRS, despite it being a binding international commitment, and the former system remains, with a controlled and circumscribed account structure within local authority accounts. This means that local authorities have not been able to use their council housing assets to fund further similar development.

Local authorities: losing the housing role

The loss of the local authority housing construction programme was brought on for a number of reasons. First, was the International Monetary Fund crisis in 1976 when the UK government sought a financial bailout (Harmon, 1997; Hickson, 2005). As a requirement of this, government capital expenditure was immediately reduced. Second, there had been a recognition that the endeavour to build more housing was missing the targets for the number of homes required both by government and to meet need (Boughton, 2018). There also continued to be a number of homeless and hidden households, as exemplified in the national consciousness through Garnett and Loach's television drama *Cathy Come Home* (1966), which led to the founding of Shelter as the leading homelessness charity (Fitzpatrick and Pawson, 2016). Third, in some locations, the construction industry had become voracious in seeking existing housing to demolish, as sites for new housing development, which had been fed by the government's dwindling housing programme. There were growing public concerns that this was leading to the redevelopment of homes that could be used with improvements and that these construction programmes were destroying communities (Davies, 1972; Garner, 1979). While the provision of new housing for people in overcrowded conditions was seen to be socially responsible, their experiences of moving to peripheral estates were culturally isolating (Johnson, 2013; Grindrod, 2017; Todd, 2019). Where new town and comprehensive development areas were the basis for new housing, there was a far greater emphasis on community development and neighbourhood units than in other council housing development (Goss, 1961; Heraud, 1973), given the extent of animosity between the people who lived in the new town locations before their creation (Wilson, 1964; Morphet, 2003). Cultural displacement was also apparent, with those in new homes often returning to their former locations to see friends and family at the weekend.

There was also a further economic change in 1976, which was turned into a political mechanism to reduce the role of local authorities in the delivery and management of social housing. This followed the agreement of the UK to sign the plurilateral Government Procurement Agreement (GPA) – under the General Agreement on Tariffs and Trade (GATT)– which was concluded as part of the Tokyo Round in 1980 (McAffee and McWilliam, 1989) and housing featured in the particular way in which successive governments decided that it should be implemented (Castellani, 2018). There had been growing concern that the market for goods was beginning to slow up and the GATT (the predecessor of the WTO) proposed, through the Tokyo Round, to introduce the opening of the public sector to private contracting (De Graaf and King, 1995; Hoekman and Mavroidis, 1995) through the GPA. This was extended from goods to include services in the Uruguay Round of the GATT that followed (1986–93), in the establishment of the General Agreement for Trade in Services (GATS).

While it is assumed that Mrs Thatcher arrived as Prime Minister in 1979 with a privatisation of public services agenda, this was not in her manifesto (Seldon and Collings, 2014). However, this manifesto did include a commitment to the sale of council houses to their existing tenants, subsequently known as Right to Buy. The introduction of RTB had longstanding roots within the policy discourse of the Conservative Party after 1945 (Jones and Murie, 2008; King, 2010; Davies, 2013). As a policy, it was immediately very successful in take-up, with some who had been tenants for more than 20 years being offered a 50% discount. By 1996, 30% of council tenants had exercised their right to buy and 2.2 million dwellings had been transferred into private ownership (Davies, 2013). Many of those who purchased their council homes in this way wanted to use their market freedoms to leave their current location and move to another location where the majority of homes were built for sale, rather than being in a community that was still associated with council housing. Councils were also not recompensed fully for the homes that were sold and not provided with any subsidies or funding to replace these homes in the public sector. As the number of council homes available for social rent was reduced, then only those with the greatest social and economic problems were eligible for these tenancies and some local authority social housing became synonymous with 'problem', workless families.

Thatcher's interest in promoting the market and her views against local government coincided with the civil service's need to propose mechanisms to implement the GATS agreement (Theakston, 1995; Gains, 1999). When each country signed the GATS agreement, they would be in a different place in terms of which public services were more available and open to competition than others. In France, for example, the role of private medical providers had been kept within the national system (Nay et al, 2016), while in Sweden, education provision had always been available to the private sector (Bunar, 2010). In each country, there was an assumption that the elements of the public sector that were least open to competition should be tackled first to reach a reasonable proportion of public expenditure opened in this way. However, it was also recognised that each signatory state would have sectors that could be politically very difficult to open to competition and that these could take some time to prepare.

In the UK, there were a number of sectors of the economy that had been nationalised after 1945, including energy and transport (Edgerton, 2011). In the implementation of the GPA, as nationalised industries were centrally controlled, these could be opened to the market by government actions and made acceptable with the electorate through a programme of popular capitalism (Jessop et al, 1988). However, other sectors might be less attractive to the market and also be less acceptable to the public. In local government, local authorities had been reorganised in 1972 (implemented in 1974) to create larger units to cope with the legislation and delivery that would follow from the UK's membership of the European Union (EU). This meant that newly expanded local authority services would be more difficult to put to the market when communities had only recently been through major changes in the structure of their local authorities. A similar issue was faced by government in the education and health sectors, which were regarded by the electorate as core government functions and where government ownership was central to the operation and ethos of these institutions. In the creation of the National Health Service (NHS), the role of general practitioners (GPs) had always been retained as contracted within the system (Majeed and Buckman, 2016) but no market existed within secondary health care before the government introduced the purchaser–provider split (Maynard, 1991). In social care there was a more mixed market as some residential homes were always provided by the private sector although many were also provided by local authorities alongside sheltered housing.

The opportunity for the introduction of competition into local government was regarded as challenging for the civil service (Ascher, 1987). There was a strong public understanding of the role of local authorities in providing local public services, which would need to be altered if the private sector was to be allowed to run some of them (Walsh, 1995). However, the prevailing ideology of Thatcher and some members of her government such as Nicholas Ridley meant that there could be an alignment between meeting international trade obligations and political rhetoric (Ridley,

1991). The approach in local government was two-fold. First, the government introduced encouragement for the development of municipal Toryism (Butcher et al, 1990). This was undertaken by encouraging those Conservative-controlled councils that supported their priorities, particularly in former Labour-controlled inner-city local authorities such as Wandsworth (where the Conservatives had won control of the council from Labour in 1978), through enhanced funding regimes and subsidies (Travers, 2015).

A second approach was used to introduce the commitments that the UK had made through the adoption of the international treaties for the GPA in 1980 and the GATS in 1994 (Morphet, forthcoming). This was to find specific ways in which the market could be introduced into local government services. This was undertaken by the introduction of the regime of compulsory competitive tendering (CCT) (Painter, 1991) and required local authorities to put defined services into a competitive tendering regime, which was based on local authorities having to accept the lowest-price tenders for the services defined in the tender specification. The focus on the lowest price as the only means through which tenders should be judged was a specific decision by the government. The GATT/WTO GPA did not require a lowest-price approach to be preferred and also offered a second social value/quality approach, which was favoured by other governments as a preferred outcome (Watermeyer, 2004). This had also been translated into the EU procurement directives (Kuijper, 1995), which were the primary legal means for implementing the GPA and GATS in the UK (Semple, 2012). The GPA and GATS required that the method being used to evaluate tenders for works or services – whether based on price or social value – had to be specified at the outset, with clear criteria being established for the preferred approach.

There were also government expectations that existing staff delivering services would not have a right to a job in any services once contracted out. However, both of these approaches were tested by local authorities. The government was required to implement the transfer of staff, including their pension rights, into the new privatised services through the application of Transfer of Undertakings (Protection of Employment) Regulations (Kerr and Radford, 1994; Adnett and Hardy, 1998). Second, local authorities eventually understood that quality could be a mechanism for determining contract tenders as well as price and started to use this method. By 2013, 80% of local authorities responding to a survey actively took considerations of economic, social and environmental wellbeing and impact into account in tender evaluation (Jackson and Harrison, 2013). This approach has taken much longer for central government to adopt in its own contracting processes. The application of CCT included direct service organisations for construction, maintenance (including for housing), cleansing and school meals – that is, the manual jobs in local government. This was followed by the intended application of CCT in the professional roles such as finance, but this was replaced by the Labour government's introduction of 'best value' (McAdam and Walker, 2004).

The second stage of this policy was to introduce the market into local authority housing provision and delivery (Spencer, 1995). By removing capital budgets for housing construction and introducing RTB policies for tenants, the local authority role was reduced and undermined immediately (Jones and Murie, 2008; Murie, 2016). Councils no longer had any funding to build more homes or maintain them using its own labour force. Further, the introduction of RTB was initially an atomised approach to marketisation but quickly became a cumulative mass transfer of public stock into the private sector. The government also introduced other financial inducements to shift the public housing stock off local authority balance sheets through stock transfer to existing or new housing associations (Malpass and Mullins, 2002). However, despite removing the ways that local authorities could provide and maintain housing directly, local authorities remained responsible for homelessness and meeting local needs, even during austerity (Loopstra et al, 2016).

Eventually, much of the RTB stock was sold into the privately rented sector and made available on the market to both private renters and local authorities (Horner, 2017). Many councils now rent the accommodation that they formerly owned to meet their homelessness obligations. At the same time, other methods of providing affordable housing failed to meet the gaps created. Initially, housing associations provided some of the accommodation in this market but increasingly they became incentivised by the government and their financial backers to provide housing for sale. A further approach was to use planning policies to provide affordable homes through developer contributions (Burgess et al, 2007; Morrison and Burgess, 2014). However, these were inadequate to meet the number of homes required and the contributions were residualised after other forms of contributions were taken for example for education. The introduction through the National Planning Policy Framework (NPPF) in 2012 (DCLG, 2012) of the notion that these contributions could not undermine the viability (that is, profitability) of developments led to a marked decline in the value of such contributions. These other forms of contribution were also more attractive to both developers and potential house purchasers as they should improve the sale price of dwellings, whereas affordable and social rented housing reduced the sale price (Morphet and Clifford, 2019).

Planning's changing role in providing housing

There has been a long association between the delivery of housing by local authorities and their role in applying planning regulation to the use of land and buildings. The Housing, Town Planning, &c. Act 1919 (often called the 'Addison Act' after the-then Minister of Health responsible for it) recognised that the role of land in providing housing and its designation was critical to enable local authorities to deliver housing. Further, the compulsory purchase of land had grown in use in the late 19th century and its role developed during the First World War for military purposes. After this, in association with the Addison Act, Compulsory Purchase Orders (CPOs) for land were considered to be an essential element in housing delivery, particularly by local authorities. In order to progress a CPO, there needed to be a planning scheme for the land that had a specific purpose and approval. This approach was continued until the Town and Country Planning Act 1947, when the introduction of comprehensive development areas for major bomb damage and improvement replacement schemes for home and town centres were introduced as central elements of housing delivery (Bullock, 2002). There were also CPOs to create new port and harbour areas (Essex and Brayshay, 2008). The provision of new towns led by central government also relied on CPOs and started to create a major government land bank. In new towns this acquired land was intended to be passed on to the local authorities within which the new towns were located when they were completed but this did not occur and much of the land in new towns is still owned by central government, now through Homes England, the government's housing agency (Hall et al, 2006).

By the mid-1960s, there was increasing public opposition to the demolition of housing through the use of comprehensive development areas and for housing development (Burns, 1963; Allen, 2008). The Skeffington (1969) report, *People and planning* proposed that there should be more public involvement and there were reforms to the planning system in 1968. This moved away from detailed land-use plans that were similar to those in use in many European countries, towards more policy-led structure and local plans where the economic, social and environmental wellbeing of any area was to be expressed spatially in more general ways (Solesbury, 2013). There was still the potential to use a more detailed approach to area change, particularly for housing renewal (Bailey and Robinson, 1997), but the expectation that the local authority would use the planning system as a mechanism for the direct delivery of its proposal using the CPO or other land acquisition and then direct implementation was lost.

These planning reforms of the late 1960s were considered to be failing to support the delivery of market sector housing while local authority plan-making was only slowly being achieved across the country. The planning reforms of 1990 and 1991 introduced what was called a 'plan-led' system where the local plan identified the land to be used for designated numbers of dwellings to be constructed (McDonald, 1997; Bingham, 2001). The government also introduced a mechanism of regional planning guidance (Glasson and Marshall, 2007). This identified and then distributed the regional strategic housing needs between local authorities and allowed local politicians the opportunity to blame central government targets for unpopular local decisions about housebuilding. As this system developed there was no provision for the delivery of affordable housing by local authorities to replace those properties lost into the private sector through RTB included in the process. Following the removal of the local authorities from the provisions of social housing, these were initially replaced by housing associations, which provided social rented housing although not to the same extent. The government supported the private sector housebuilding industry and increasingly housing decisions were being taken using planning appeals rather than being provided through sites identified in local plans (Ball, 2011; Gurran and Bramley, 2017). However, although homelessness and a lack of affordable housing continued to be an issue for local authorities, provision for this was increasingly marginalised in the planning system.

The 1997 Labour government concentrated on the reform of local government in its first term and did not focus on planning reforms until its second term of office (Morphet, 2007). In the Local Government Act 2000, each local authority was required to prepare a Sustainable Community Strategy in conjunction with its partners (Williams, 2002;

Raco et al, 2006). A Government planning Green Paper (ODPM, 2001) issued shortly before the 2001 general election closely connected the new approach of Sustainable Community Strategies to the preparation of a local plan, giving them a delivery focus and making them central to the local authority's mission. This approach was carried through into the Planning and Compulsory Purchase Act 2004, where a new approach to spatial planning was introduced, combining policy with delivery and set with the council's community strategy (Morphet, 2004; Tewdwr Jones et al, 2006). The 2004 Act also introduced new approaches to establishing regional planning guidance – the Regional Spatial Strategies – which again offered the opportunity for local authorities to share the market housing requirements between them (Morphet, 2011).

While this approach was set within the EU approaches to innovative government models that included the community and integrated local strategies and delivery programmes (Moulaert et al, 2005), there were also central government concerns about the volume of housing being built. In a policy review, the Chancellor of the Exchequer invited economist Kate Barker to report on the ways in which more housing could be provided. Barker's (2004) first report identified the role of the planning system as being more central to the provision of housing than other government policy interventions, for example fiscal policy, and this led to a second review of land-use planning led by Barker in 2006 (Barker, 2006). In her work, Barker assumed that affordable housing would be provided by subsidies given to local authorities by the government. However, in practice, her reviews introduced an expectation that assumed that affordable and social housing would be a residual outcome from other development, provided by developers' contributions (Crook et al, 2006; Corkindale, 2007). While the development market was strong, then there were possibilities that local authorities might be able to use these development contribution negotiations as a means of providing this social housing. However, as studies of the application of these negotiated agreements to seek these developer contributions evidence, these approaches varied in their use by local authorities (Morrison and Burgess, 2014; Burgess and Monk, 2016). Some councils did not require any contributions as part of the planning system as they considered that it might be a disincentive to potential housebuilders. Others asked for small contributions or, if housing schemes were won by housing developers on appeal, the local authorities had not included contributions as part of the requirement and hence did not receive any for the development when built. Some developers also used experts to argue down contributions (McAllister et al, 2018).

While these attempts to implement and provide social and affordable housing through planning contributions were being pursued, the housebuilding industry was continuing to press government for an easier and more deregulated planning system. Initially after the economic crisis in 2007, many development companies divested their land assets and reduced their housebuilding to a very low level. When the coalition government was elected in 2010, there was sympathy for developers' arguments for a reform of the planning system. The government introduced the Localism Act 2011 as part of this process, accompanied by the NPPF (DCLG, 2012), which changed the nature of planning decision making in both plans and for individual applications, and in 2015 the government established the Local Plan Expert Group to report on the system. Following this, supported by the Prime Minister's housing adviser (Morton, 2010, 2016), after 2015 the Conservative government reduced much of the planning system to make it easier to obtain planning consent (Clifford et al, 2019). Local authorities were also incentivised to provide more homes, through the provision of a New Homes Bonus for every completed dwelling, while housing developers were supported through market incentives to buyers through the Help to Buy scheme (Hiber, 2013; Finlay et al, 2016).

Planning is not enough to deliver housing

The pressures of austerity and homelessness started to stimulate local authorities into considering more direct action (Morphet, 2016). After ten years of austerity (Toynbee and Walker, 2020) and the increased deregulation in the planning system, local authorities were seeking new ways of providing housing that were not reliant on the planning system for delivery. The government also started to recognise that it should reconsider how housing is provided and did this through the publication of a White Paper (MHCLG, 2017). The agency created by government to support the delivery of housing took over the Housing Corporation and became responsible for the funding and oversight of housing associations. This was the Homes and Communities Agency (HCA). In 2011, it appeared that the HCA was being run down but by 2017 its local roles had been translated into a national body, Homes England, with a £32 billion budget.

The housing White Paper (MHCLG, 2017) also gave local authorities more confidence to assess their own roles in housing provision. For the first time since 1980, the paper appeared to give more positive support to councils providing housing (Morphet and Clifford, 2017). The introduction of the Homelessness Reduction Act 2017 placed greater responsibilities on all local authorities to help households avoid homelessness. The government has not, however, placed any restrictions on landlord behaviours, even though there is considerable evidence of a rise in no-fault evictions (Hudak, 2018; Cowan, 2019; Simcock and McKee, 2019).

Housing as local government's core mission

The relationship between local authorities and the direct provision of housing is a complex one. For central government, the role of local authorities in providing housing in a consistent and controlled way at specific times has been one of client and contractor. Local authorities have never been part of the UK constitution and while, for a period before 1945, they were largely self-financing through the levy of local property taxes, in the post-war period their role expanded to provide public services to deliver government priorities, which largely coincided with their own. This required an increase in their size and capacity, which, in turn, made them dependent on funding from central government. However, while local authorities were delivering social housing for government in these contracted arrangements, the housing that was then provided was strongly associated with the local authority's core role. With greater provision of housing also came a need for management and maintenance to support those new dwellings, which further developed the relationships between councils and citizens.

In some local authorities, particularly those with poorer socioeconomic characteristics, the scale of council house provision grew as a percentage of all housing types. In the London Borough of Tower Hamlets in 1976, 98% of housing was publicly provided by the Greater London Council or the borough (Low, 1983). In Bristol, the council owns 50% of the land that is used for housing in the city. As council housing moved from being a main type of tenure in many local authorities to one regarded as a place of last resort for homelessness, with market housing taking over as a preferred option, larger estates became ghettoised (Forrest and Murie, 1983; Hancock and Mooney, 2013). Councils no longer have the funds for management and maintenance onsite and community norms for social control have been reduced (Haworth and Manzi, 1999; Saugeres, 2000). This was recognised as a major issue and target for public policy in the early 2000s by the Blair government (HM Treasury, 2004), although the scale of response was not accompanied by a repositioning of esteem for council housing as a mainstream form of housing tenure for households in work. Instead, governments have continued to prioritise policies that align with elector preferences for homeownership over renting and where renting council housing is seen as being synonymous with poverty and need (Ball, 1983).

Conclusions

Although the provision of housing by local government can be regarded as operating as a contracted relationship between central and local government over the past 100 years, for many local authorities it became their defined role after other services such as energy provision and public health were removed. It provided a sense of pride in the delivery of new homes, there was an opportunity for some wider community patronage and it enabled councils to demonstrate positive social action towards their residents. The delivery of housing was also an important service for the support of existing and new businesses. People who were well housed in affordable homes that were healthy and well heated provided a constant supply for the local labour market. While other council services were important such as education, not all households had children of school age and similarly with the needs of older people who required specialist housing and care. Local government provision of housing also provided the expectation to families that their children would be able to find housing in the area and stay close by (Grindrod, 2017). If children lived at home and did not set up their own households, they could expect the tenancy to be passed on to them. All these practices helped people feel secure, supported and valued within the local area.

Since the local authority housing responsibilities have been diminished, there has been a residual interest in returning to this role, expressed by councillors when facing election. Communities often do not understand why councils cannot provide housing when housing developers have been apparently able to build new housing relatively easily. The planning system has appeared to favour the private sector while it was not doing the same for the public sector. The government's definition of affordable housing, provided through the planning system, did not seem to match what communities considered to be affordable rents. The loss of the role of housing delivery undermined the confidence of local authorities and none of the powers or services remaining to them appeared to offer a positive contribution to their sense of value and worth. The residualisation of local authority functions to regulatory roles for planning, council tax collection, housing benefits, parking or licensing did not seem to reach out to the whole community. The extent of austerity applied from 2010 removed many of the positive services that were left – libraries, community development, youth services and leisure. Thatcherism removed the roles of local authorities using legal means and a highly interventionist approach (Butcher et al, 1990). The austerity period has had the effect of making local authorities remove their own services: they could blame central government for the cuts, but they had to make the specific choices about which services to lose or reduce. These direct decisions have had the effect of suggesting poorer local management rather than communicating the effects of government budget cuts.

The loss of the council's housing role has also contributed to the diminution of community and social cohesion. The provision of social housing helped local authorities take responsibility for a large part of their population. While Thatcher argued that that was a patronising position and that people should be able to exercise more free choice over housing, the accompanying housing finance system has not left open the opportunities of that choice for all the population. The role of the private sector in housing provision has also brought specific problems for local authorities in respect of design and space standards. Much of this housing has small room sizes, is finished poorly and can frequently have locked-in leasehold arrangements that make the housing difficult to sell. Faced with these issues, the housing is not sold to those who will be resident but goes immediately to the buy-to-let market with short-term tenancies. The new housing estates are not designed with this tenure in mind and there are few provisions for housing maintenance and the management of the public realm. Some new developments appear to move from completion to sink estate status very rapidly. When trying to find housing for homeless people, councils may have to use these properties, paying high rent rates to the owners. In some councils that have contemplated purchase of new developments to add to their own stock, this has been rejected as the new properties are not considered to be of adequate size and finish for the councils to take into their management.

For all of these reasons, local authorities have started to re-engage with the direct provision of housing. Rather than reducing local authority confidence and roles further, the government's distraction over Brexit and the pressures of austerity have encouraged councils to find new ways of providing services and generating income. It has also helped in beginning to restore local authority confidence. We explore these motivations further in the next chapter.

THREE

Challenging austerity: why have local authorities been taking their own action?

Introduction

Local authorities in England have been intimately involved in the twin crises of super-austerity and housing over the past decade. And as John (2014: 688) has written, 'repeated pronouncements of the end or terminal decline of locally elected government should be treated very cautiously'. Local government 'remains a remarkable site for contestations and debate … (still around some of the same things as always – the delivery of care services, the fight for decent housing and so on)' (Ward et al, 2015: 453). In the context of the remarkably resilient and adaptive system of local government in England, there has been a pushback by authorities against austerity and in favour of their own direct action in delivering housing. In this chapter, focusing on local authorities' direct role in housing delivery, we consider what has motivated them to get engaged in direct delivery again in recent years, including frustrations at private developers within the planning system, and the forms of provision to deal with homelessness, housing and income generation and how these are enabled legislatively.

We draw extensively on our own empirical research, reported in Morphet and Clifford (2017, 2019). For the 2017 research this included 13 roundtable discussions held across England, 12 case study interviews with local authority officers and politicians, a direct survey (online questionnaire) sent by email to local authority officers, which resulted in a total of 268 responses from officers working in 197 different local authorities across England (sent in 2017), and a desk survey of online information about local authority housing delivery activity. For the 2019 research this included a further 13 roundtable discussions held across England, 13 case study interviews with local authority officers and politicians, a direct survey sent by email to local authority officers, which resulted in 184 responses from officers working in 142 different local authorities across England (sent in 2018), and a new desk survey of online information about housing delivery activity by every local authority in England, focusing particularly on housing and property companies.

Local authority motivations

We have found through our research that local authorities directly engaging in housing delivery, do so for a wide variety of reasons that vary between authorities. A particular council has often come to the direct delivery of housing with one specific motivation, wanting to tackle a particular local issue, but then realised that engaging in this activity might address several different issues. Perhaps the best way to characterise this incremental engagement with sites and provision of housing is 'problem solving'. Many local authorities have started with an issue and concluded that direct engagement with housing provision would be an answer, which they then decide to pursue. Subsequently, they start to consider other problems or sites and this leads them to extend their repertoire of interventions.

Table 3.1: Motivating factors for local authorities to engage directly in housing provision, in order of importance according to survey respondents

Factor	2017 importance rank	2018 importance rank
To meet housing requirements	1	1
To tackle homelessness	2	2
Income generation	3	= 3
To improve quality of design	8	= 3
Because local authorities should be building housing	9	= 5
Place regeneration (for example, town centre)	= 6	= 5
Estate regeneration	4	= 5
Private sector build-out rates are too slow	5	8
To deal with problem sites	10	9
To change public perceptions of place	11	10
Frustration at unimplemented planning permissions	= 6	11
To support small business	12	12

In our two direct surveys, we asked local authority respondents to rank the importance of their motivating factors to be involved in the direct provision of housing (having identified motivators from our initial roundtable discussions). Table 3.1 illustrates the answers from both surveys.

Perhaps unsurprisingly, comparison between the 2017 and 2018 surveys reveals that meeting local housing requirements, tackling homelessness and income generation remain the top three motivations for local authorities in the direct provision of housing. Indeed, the income generation motivator is the key link between the housing crisis and the austerity crisis. There are then a range of other issues that remain important to authorities and are motivating them to engage in direct delivery. Notably, the desire to improve design quality has apparently become a much more important motivator for local authorities. The notion that local authorities should be building housing also gained importance as a motivator between the 2017 and 2018 surveys, while frustration at unimplemented consents and private sector build-out rates dropped in importance for local authorities. They do remain key motivators for some authorities, however, as do a wider range of other different factors such as place making, estate regeneration and supporting local small and medium-sized enterprises (such as local builders).

Considering these in more detail, the main reason given by local authorities for returning to providing housing directly is because they wish to meet local housing requirements. Local need and demand are often high, evidenced in housing strategies and local plans and demonstrated by local market conditions and housing waiting lists. In some areas of the country, there then seems to be market failure in that there has been little or no private developer interest at all in building on sites in their areas – particularly in rural areas. Councils regard provision of housing as a basic service they should provide and have never really become accustomed to the removal of this role, which has been one with a long history (as discussed in Chapter Two). These councils include the 48% of councils that have retained a social housing function through the HRA. It is also considered to be an important council function by the electorate, who see rising housing problems and consider that it is a legitimate role for local authorities to engage directly in meeting these needs. These councils have also been considering other ways in which the skills of their development teams can be used and expanded to provide a wider range of housing including of different types and tenures. Communities often see local authorities as having a core role as housing providers, and local councillors have provided some political drive and ambition around returning to this function in many places.

Linked to this is a concern that even where the private sector is developing, there is a mismatch between their primarily market-sale housing delivery and local need. This may be about particular types of housing, such as that suitable for older or disabled people. Indeed, in our 2018 survey we found that 71% of respondents reported that their local authority was building or planning to build housing for older people specifically. This compared to 42% in 2017. Other particular needs were also being addressed, with 37% of councils building housing for people with mental health problems and 60% for people with physical disabilities. More broadly, however, it is frequently about affordable housing. This may be due to difficulties in negotiating affordable homes as planning contributions as part of wider development, the renegotiation of these agreements once concluded or the crowding out of affordable housing due to requirements for other social infrastructure (Gibb, 2018; Wyatt, 2018; Clegg and Farstad, 2019; Gurran, 2019). Further the introduction of viability tests for contributions for planning applications incorporating housing development has reduced the volume of funding available and the provision of affordable housing is in competition with other infrastructure and is residual. At the same time, there has been an increased level of developer renegotiation of viability tests and contributions after planning consents have been granted, which again has reduced the level of contributions made. This has been counteracted in those councils that have applied clawback provisions to these planning consents, but this is by no means universal across the country. Clawback provisions in developer agreements allow the contributions agreed at the outset to be set within a final settlement based on sale prices achieved as recorded by the Land Registry, but even these are not always successful (Burgess and Monk, 2016).

The delivery of affordable housing has been a pressing concern for many local authorities. As already discussed in Chapter Two, since the 1980s the UK has been increasingly reliant on the private sector for the delivery of housing, but private providers are – understandably – usually motivated by profit rather than public good. At the same time, housing itself (as discussed in Chapter One), has increasingly become seen within the UK economy as an asset defined by its exchange value rather than a social good defined by its use value. This has meant that housing is increasingly expensive, and unaffordable for much of society. The number of council homes has also declined due to the RTB policy. With stock transfer (originating in the late 1980s but mainly encouraged from 2000 to 2008), there has been a key role for housing associations in providing new affordable housing, but with mergers and funding issues, delivery does not match demand in many places, and this has been a source of frustration to many local authorities.

The current dominant idea in English planning is that affordable housing can be delivered as a residual of market housing, through private developers funding units through a negotiated Section 106 agreement. The supply provided through this route has not always been truly affordable (depending on the definition used and agreement over tenure mix during negotiations) nor has it usually matched demand. The number of units delivered also sharply declined following the 2012 NPPF (DCLG, 2012) and associated 2012 Planning Practice Guidance, which clearly stated that such Section 106 contributions could not be required if they made the development unviable, with a mini-industry growing up around the production of such viability assessments (McAllister et al, 2016; Crosby and Wyatt, 2016). The base assumption that a developer should make a 20% profit margin before delivering affordable housing under Section 106 has led many local authorities to wonder whether they could deliver housing themselves and then utilise that profit margin for a social purpose, through delivering a greater amount of affordable housing and/or delivering income to fund other council services.

The percentage of new-build homes that are classed by the government as affordable housing declined from being 40% of units in 2010–11 to being 16% in 2015–16, albeit there has been some increase recently, to 23% in 2018–19 (MHCLG, 2019b). In 2018–19, 82% of these new affordable homes were delivered by registered providers, like housing associations (this had been 96% in 1999–2000), with local authorities delivering 11% (this was 0.002% in 1999–2000 – 58 units out of 35,091). Forty-nine per cent of new affordable housing units delivered in 2018–19 were funded by Section 106 (nil grant) agreements. Looking at government statistics, it is particularly noticeable that there has been a sharp drop in the number of new social rent units being constructed, from 39,562 in 2010–11 to 6,287 in 2018–19 (MHCLG, 2019b). The need for more truly affordable housing provision has been a motivator for local authorities to try to engage with the direct delivery of housing again, but also, through the growing focus on viability, there has been an increasing awareness of the profits that have been made by some private developers through housebuilding, and also some housing associations (where acting more as market developers) and this also interests local authorities.

In some places, meeting local housing need is also impacted by second homes and student housing accounting for part of the take-up of existing supply. While second homes are regarded as being a key issue in some parts of the country such as the south west, they are also emerging as a key driver in motivating local authorities to provide housing stock in other areas where second homes are prevalent such as outer London. For student housing, we were told of locations where supply is outstripping demand but that while this type of development appears to provide a guaranteed income as it is not currently subject to stamp duty, this remains a very popular type of new development. There are also councils dealing with student accommodation in houses in multiple occupation, where standards and conditions require increased regulation. Local residents may not welcome the consequent changes in their areas.

The planning system has also failed to provide the range of housing needed. Morphet and Clifford (2019) found that in many councils there is a considerable mismatch between the type of housing identified through housing need assessments and that identified through the planning system. In the government's approaches to housing delivery through the planning system, there has been a focus on the provision of market housing for sale and more recently with the addition of market housing for rent. Following the publication of the NPPF in 2012 (DCLG, 2012) and the updates to it in 2018/19 (MHCLG, 2019c), local authorities are required to identify five- to seven-year land supply for these types of market housing. While the 2019 version of the NPPF offers local authorities the opportunity to identify their requirements for special needs housing, this is not supported by the same method of allocating sites that is used for market housing in the planning system. If all the market housing need has been met, the government system does not allow local authorities to retain the remaining housing sites for the other needs that have been identified and these too have to be used for market-sale or rented housing. Local authorities have therefore returned to providing homes as a response to the failures in the planning system to provide the type of housing that is needed in their local areas.

The second driver that has brought local authorities into the direct provision of housing is through their duties to avoid and respond to homelessness, as set out in the Homelessness Reduction Act 2017. This applies to all councils, whether or not they have a retained housing function, and has led to councils without an HRA to start to invest in purchasing housing stock either directly or through the use of companies. This has also been stimulated by the rising levels and costs of homelessness due to an increase in no-fault evictions. The use of accommodation created from former factories and offices through the extension of permitted development rights has added to the stock but much of this is small and in inappropriate locations for families such as on industrial estates (Clifford et al, 2019). The costs of meeting homelessness primarily through renting properties on the private market was £1 billion in 2017 (NAO, 2017), prior to the new duties being introduced. After the Homelessness Reduction Act was introduced in practice in 2018, costs in London alone increased to £919 million (London Councils, 2019; Wilson and Barton, 2019). There are also significant social costs resulting from homelessness for children who have little space to undertake their homework. Families are also located at some distance from families and friends and from jobs (McPhillips, 2017). Councils, such as in South Cambridgeshire, are purchasing properties on the open market to increase their local stock or are buying elsewhere. In some cases, where it also meets wider estate management objectives, councils are purchasing former RTB properties to return them to their stock. For some councils, these house purchases are by one of their wholly owned companies and the day-to-day management and maintenance of these properties may be undertaken under contract by other providers, including other local authorities (LGA, 2017b) and housing associations (LGA and NHF, 2019).

For some councils that are using housing purchase and development to generate income, then there is a focus on building at least some housing for sale. The third main reason for local authorities engaging in housing provision has been to generate income to replace the Revenue Support Grant (RSG), which has been tapered out between 2012 and 2020. Councils have found funding before to support their wider services and activities through asset sales but as interest rates are low, in the longer term, generating consistent and rising revenue streams that reflect growing demand and inflation through rents and property taxes provides a more secure form of income on which to base service provision. Local authorities are using a variety of methods to secure property to provide rental income. In some cases, local authorities are developing their own housing either directly through their general fund or through some form of company, which may be preferred as it provides tax advantages and therefore more income.

In some areas, on Teesside for example, councils have been developing homes for sale for the executive end of the housing market, either to meet a local housing need not being met by developers or to increase their council tax income through the creation of a greater proportion of higher council tax band properties. In some areas, this has been described as 'council tax farming' (Cain, 2018) and has led to changes in political control at local elections (Tighe and Bounds, 2019). Some councils are adding to their property portfolio through the purchase of housing for market rent outside their local authority areas, while others are purchasing commercial developments that provide a rental income in the same way as institutional pension providers. In these cases, the local authority is moving to characterise its role as a patient investor, investing its capital funding to generate longer-term income. There has been some criticism in the press of local authorities taking this approach, suggesting that purchasing assets of this kind is a considerable risk. However, this has been countered by those who reject this view, saying that these investments are backed with assets that can be resold or developed in the future.

Concerns about the quality of housing delivered were, in our most recent survey, the joint-third most common motivator for local authorities engaging directly with housing provision again (with a sharp increase in importance between our two surveys). A high degree of frustration has been expressed by local authorities about the internal design and space standards of private sector-led housing development, and along with a willingness to engage with higher-quality standards, such as Passivhaus and energy efficiency. Given completely free reign over design matters through deregulated permitted development, certain private developers have delivered housing units marked by extremely small space standards and poor access to daylight, even without any windows at all in some cases (Clifford et al, 2019).

Beyond the extremes of permitted development, however, there are more widespread issues with the design and quality of much new development coming through the planning system, which the government has also recognised as being a significant issue (MHCLG, 2019a). A recent audit by Place Alliance looking at 142 large-scale housing development projects across England concluded that, across a range of 17 design considerations, three quarters were 'mediocre' or 'poor' and a fifth were so bad they should have been refused planning permission (Place Alliance, 2020).

We have been told that there have been cases where housing associations have refused units delivered through Section 106 contributions from private developers as the space standards are so poor and that design quality can also include the finishing of new properties. With the homes delivered through the negotiation of affordable homes as part of development contributions sometimes so small or badly finished, meaning that housing associations will not take them, the local authority has then directly taken on the ownership and management responsibilities. In other cases, councils have considered purchasing completed market homes to meet their needs but have not done so in practice when the room sizes of the properties have been considered against their own standard.

There is thus a strong objective among some local authorities to demonstrate to the private sector that housing can be designed well, be compliant with local plan policies/standards and be delivered. This also demonstrates the demand for high-quality housing. Local authorities have also said they are pursuing this approach as a means of providing an uplift to areas through the role of design in creating places. Where local authorities are motivated by this approach, they are using external design teams working to briefs set by the council.

Planning concerns are, in various ways, another strong motivator for local authorities to engage in the direct delivery of housing. First, there is still an issue nationally with unimplemented planning consents, albeit with concerted action by local authorities, although this appears to be reducing in importance as a motivating factor. Research from the Local Government Association published in 2018 found that there were unimplemented planning permissions in England and Wales that would involve the construction of 423,544 new homes (The Planner, 2018). The same report noted that local authorities had approved 321,202 homes in 2016/17 compared with 204,989 in 2015/16 but that the time taken for completion had increased to 40 months, on average, after permission was granted. As a result, the Local Government Association argued that planning is not a barrier to housebuilding per se, that the private sector could not provide the widely cited requirement of 300,000 homes per annum in England alone and that instead councils needed to be supported to build housing directly (The Planner, 2018). Such issues do indeed act as a motivator for local authorities building housing again, particularly when councillors on planning committees sometimes feel they have taken difficult decisions approving schemes, possibly against some local opposition, only to then not see anything actually built.

The reduction in amelioration benefits provided as part of the planning consent and the slow build-out rates that maintain price levels (Letwin, 2018) have both been a political and community concern. When local politicians discuss potential housing development with existing residents, the promise of new infrastructure can make the proposals more palatable. However, when these are reduced or removed through renegotiation, both the politicians and the community feel that they have been let down by developers and this makes them more wary when further development is proposed. Local authorities are beginning to deal with this through overage and clawback clauses within Section 106 agreements, which see a return to the council if a price achieved for a sale is higher than that agreed in the viability assessment. However, this approach does not help deal with issues related to slow build-out rates, particularly that the housing is not available for those who need it. Slow build-out rates can also be a source of community antagonism if construction traffic is using local roads for many years. Letwin (2018) found that larger sites were subject to slower build-out rates that extended in some cases beyond 15 years.

Place regeneration can also be another factor linking local authority planning and motivation to engagement in the direct delivery of housing. Many local authorities are undertaking regeneration schemes either for their own housing or in town centres where they own land. The motivation to undertake this kind of activity is to improve the council's assets and to increase housing supply. In some cases, these approaches are resulting in major redevelopment and changes in land use. In others, which are more usually characterised as hidden home initiatives, small areas such as garages are being redeveloped for housing. If the scheme involves the redevelopment of existing social housing estates, there may be an element of using market housing development to renew social housing, and this can be particularly controversial (for example, Beswick and Penny, 2018). More broadly, some local authorities are motivated to invest in housing development as a means of changing perceptions of their place. In this case they may be building housing of varied sizes and scales of area where other changes in land-use demand have freed up sites for major change. Changing the perception of a city or town also has the potential to increase other investment and to encourage graduates to remain in their university town to set up businesses or work in local organisations and companies. Many local authorities are also concerned with the quality of the existing housing stock whether owned by the public or private sector. In the private sector, there are concerns about management by local landlords and some local authorities are pursuing licensing vigorously.

Finally, council involvement in housing delivery has sometimes been motivated by a desire to support local small builders and architects and the creation of apprenticeships. Many local authorities wish to support local small businesses, especially builders and those in the supply chain in their areas. Through generating a range of housing developments on small- and medium-sized sites, smaller builders and developers can bid for this work. We were also advised that local authority work is beneficial in market downturns as it is less affected by these shifts. Local authorities are also trying to support apprenticeships. This might include requiring all builders and contractors working for them to support apprenticeships and training as part of their overall procurement approaches, or through the council itself having apprenticeship programmes associated with its company or housing development activity in-house.

Forms of provision, legal powers and funding

Local authorities motivated to deliver housing directly can use a wide range of approaches. However, the most common are building under the HRA, building through their general fund and building through a wholly owned or joint venture council company. A local authority that has retained its housing stock will have an HRA and, under the auspices of the Housing Act 1985 and Local Government and Housing Act 1989, may use funds in the HRA to build further housing. This is ordinarily the route to building replacement socially rented 'council housing'. The local authority may also finance the building of any tenure of housing directly from its general fund (the council's account excluding the HRA), which is underpinned by its general powers to promote the economic, environmental or social wellbeing of its area under the Local Government Act 2000. Anyone considered to be a council tenant for homes built through these routes would potentially be able to exercise their right to buy the property at a substantial discount.

In 2012, there were 169 local authorities across England that had retained their housing stock, rather than transferring it to a social provider like a housing association (which was encouraged by the 1997–2010 Labour government). For a number of years, rents collected from such council housing were centrally pooled; however, by the end of the Labour government, these were permitted to be locally retained. The HRA takes its income from rents and service charges collected from tenants and the council can then spend this money only on building and maintaining housing. The council can borrow money against the value of its assets – the housing stock – to refurbish or build more council housing; however, the coalition government introduced a strict cap on such borrowing in April 2012, much less than the value of the assets, in order to try to control public borrowing (Barker, 2018). In October 2018, the-then Prime Minister Theresa May announced that the cap was being lifted, so that authorities could borrow more in order to build more housing. A majority of councils that retained stock reported that this would allow them to build more new housing and they intended to do so (LGA, 2019b); however, this does not benefit the majority of authorities that do not retain stock. Further, there is not much evidence, as yet, that this has been taken up by many councils. The provision of housing through the HRA is still at 'risk' of being lost from the council's social housing stock from RTB and many councils now prefer to use some of the other methods of providing housing that are open to them.

All local councils are, however, able to benefit from what John (2014) argues are additional freedoms and flexibility brought about by the coalition government, such as the power of general competence. Sections 1 to 7 of the Localism Act 2011 allow a local authority to do anything an individual might do, including setting up a company for commercial purposes. Ferry et al (2018) highlight the way that the creation of local authority companies is a growing phenomenon across the whole of English local government and believe this is a significant development in relation to governance, performance and efficiency. They call the creation of local authority companies a process of 'corporatisation' and note that while there is a long history of municipal corporations, the power to trade local authority services commercially under the Local Government Act 2003 and the ability to undertake any activity unless specifically prohibited by statute under the Localism Act 2011 have led to highly favourable conditions for the establishment of a range of local authority corporate forms, which may then be utilised to generate new revenue streams and take a more flexible approach to employment and reward systems than has been the case within local authorities directly. For our purposes, as we will see in Chapter Four, the ability to establish a company has been widely used in relation to property investment and housing development.

Although our focus is on England, it is worth noting that what Vroon et al (2017) say that 'municipally owned corporations' are increasingly seen across Europe, with municipalities in Germany, Italy and the Netherlands apparently having on average between 10 and 20 local corporations each. These have been utilised as an alternative to contracting out to the private sector, where the cost savings and benefits can diminish over time, and are flexible in form and ownership: some will be wholly owned by one council, others by a number of different councils, and some will be shared by the public and private sectors. Vroon et al (2017: 820) conclude by arguing that such companies, which can be used to provide local services, 'are often more efficient than local bureaucracies in the provision of services such as refuse collection, water distribution, and transit services, although they also have high initial failure rates. We conclude that municipally owned corporations are a viable means for delivering some local public services for localities capable of initiating and managing complex contracts'.

In terms of funding, housing built under the HRA can be funded through borrowing against the retained stock as assets and receipts from properties sold under the RTB. This is subject to certain restrictions from government: the Local Government Act 2003 imposes a three-year limit on authorities spending RTB receipts and specifies that they must fund no more than 30% of the cost of a replacement unit. Given these restrictions, 28% of respondents in our 2018 survey said their local authority was actually not using its RTB receipts to build new housing itself at all (albeit this was a reduction on the 34% who reported this in our 2017 survey).

RTB homes are sold at a significant reduction compared with market prices, and these reductions were strengthened in 2012. Local authorities have, perhaps unsurprisingly, not been building as many units as there have been losses through RTB sales (MHCLG, 2019b). Housing built under the HRA or the council's general fund can also be funded through a grant, for example from Homes England or the Mayor of London. There has also been a new initiative by the Mayor of London to support local authorities in building council housing again using £1.75 billion funding, with the objective of building 10,000 homes. Councils were invited to bid for grant funding that would allow them to build housing at council housing rents (Eichler, 2018).

In relation to local authority companies delivering housing, our own surveys asked authorities how their companies were funded. Table 3.2 summarises our findings. Overall, our findings are that local authorities are drawing on a wide range of sources of funding to support the delivery of housing. Many local authorities that are building housing again started with the HRA and then sought to find innovative additional sources. Companies that are more commercially focused (with a motivator of income generation) often utilise the Public Works Loan Board (PWLB). Most companies draw on more than one source of funding.

The PWLB is an independently managed government body and is the main source of borrowing for local government in the UK, with the purpose of allowing councils relatively low interest finance to fund local infrastructure projects and similar capital expenditure. There is an overall cap on the amount local government can borrow (£95 billion) but councils do not need

Table 3.2: How were local authority housing companies being funded?

Source of funding (the same company may draw on more than one source of funding / support)	2017 number of companies	2017 percentage of responses	2018 number of companies	2018 percentage of responses
Public Works Loan Board	40	13.7%	29	13.0%
Council's own resources: finance	68	23.2%	47	21.1%
Council's own resources: buildings and land	59	20.1%	45	20.2%
Using council buildings for office-to-residential	6	2.0%	5	2.2%
Building on council's own land	54	18.4%	37	16.6%
Loans from other local authorities	4	1.4%	2	0.9%
Bonds	3	1.0%	0	0.0%
Commercial loans	10	3.4%	8	3.6%
Hedge fund(s)	0	7.5%	0	0.0%
European Investment Bank	0	0.7%	0	0.0%

(continued)

Table 3.2: How were local authority housing companies being funded? (continued)

Source of funding (the same company may draw on more than one source of funding / support)	2017 number of companies	2017 percentage of responses	2018 number of companies	2018 percentage of responses
Homes and Communities Agency / Homes England	22	7.5%	17	7.6%
Local enterprise partnership / devolution + city deals	2	1.0%	7	3.1%
Section 106 payments	22	13.7%	20	2.7%
From a joint venture partner	3	23.2%	*Not asked*	
Land sales	*Not asked*		6	9.0%

to specify what they will use the loans, which can last up to 50 years, for (Davies, 2019). These loans can then be passed on at a margin to the local authority's housing companies, thus making a surplus or income, through the interest paid, to support other services. The margin is required to avoid state aid rules; however, even with this, a local authority can loan its own company funds it has in turn received from the PWLB at historically low rates and/or can utilise the PWLB loans from within the general fund without any margins. The PWLB interest rates had been at a historic low of 1.8% until October 2019, when HM Treasury announced they would be increased to 2.8%, which it has been speculated was to discourage local authorities from commercial property speculation activity (Davies, 2019). LGiU and *MJ* (2020) reported that this interest rate rise meant that 59% of councils had to alter their 2020/21 financial plans, but that 87% of local authorities still planned to borrow from the PWLB during that financial year, while 23% planned to use the Municipal Bonds Agency. This shows the extent of the use of this source of funding.

Given that recently the PWLB has been offering lower than commercial interest rate loans, and we are seeing an increasing amount of activity around housebuilding and property investment by local authorities, the level of local authority loans taken from the PWLB has been increasing and was reported to have reached a seven-year high in 2018 (Brady, 2018), increasing by 42% in the 2017/18 financial year. In that year, the PWLB advanced 780 loans with a value of £5.2 billion to local authorities, compared with 622 loans with a value of £3.6 billion in 2016/17 and increasing again to 1,308 loans with a value of £9.1 billion in 2018/19 (UKDMO, 2019).

Councils have also been supporting their own companies with loans from their general fund, but also through the utilisation of council buildings and land for their activities. Land is particularly important to the story of local authority austerity and housing. As noted in Chapter One, Christophers (2018) reported the extent to which local authorities were selling their own land, allowing others to develop it (primarily for housing) and profit, but with the rise of local authority direct delivery of housing and a desire to capture some of the uplift in value to help fund council services, this situation is rapidly changing.

For those authorities directly delivering housing, according to our 2018 survey, 95% are building on their own land, 44% are purchasing sites to develop, 42% are purchasing existing residential buildings, 17% are using land from the One Public Estate initiative and 13% are using other public land. Most authorities will start with their own landownership holdings initially, given how much more viable this can obviously make schemes. For a variety of historic and institutional factors, local authority landownership varies considerably across England, but we understand that many local authorities have started to take a more detailed look at what they own and are seriously considering its development potential. In many cases, the management of land has been left to estates departments, which have not always been fully focused on the use potential of the land for providing housing or have simply seen excess land as a route to make a quick profit through selling it off rather than considering longer-term investment potential. That is now changing. A more joined-up approach involving local authority housing, planning and estates teams can help identify a much greater range of sites suitable for the council's own housing development. Once the local authority (or their company) is then well practised at housing development, they might then move from their own land to acquiring sites. Often this is done through an agent to avoid the price being inflated artificially. Our 2018 survey also shows that 61% of authorities are acquiring more land and/or buildings as part of a longer-term investment strategy to support income, acting as patient investors. This appears to be a growing trend and is quite the reversal of the situation Christophers (2017) identified, motivated strongly by an income generation goal for local authorities.

The use of the PWLB and local authorities' own land holdings are extremely important factors in how they are delivering housing again and attempting to use housebuilding to overcome austerity effects. There is, however, a much wider source of funds and support in relation to the direct delivery of housing. There appears to be an increasing trend for local authorities to take on the management of affordable housing provided through Section 106 agreements with private developers directly, rather than passing these to another registered provider like a housing association. There are a wide range of funding schemes available from Homes England, which local authorities have been drawing down on. Some devolution arrangements and associated funding allocations to combined authorities, growth deals and city deals have also been related to works to support development sites and unlock problems such as ground conditions, remediation and site investigations for strategic housing development. Commercial borrowing has also been used by some council housing companies. Beyond our survey, we did find evidence in our research of some local authorities, including the London Boroughs of Enfield and Barking and Dagenham, using the European Investment Bank to fund major housing development, although uncertainty over Brexit has discouraged other local authorities from following this route. The European Investment Bank provides loans for major public capital investment and supported housing projects in the UK over a number of years.

Conclusions

Given the challenges of super-austerity, it is perhaps unsurprising that income generation features strongly among the motivating factors for local authorities who are now re-engaging with the direct delivery of housing. Many local authorities have seen the profits made by commercial developers not only through their own engagement over planning viability agreements, but also in national headlines about the extremely high level of profits made by some volume housebuilders in England (NAO 2019), and they thought that there is an opportunity to help fund services ravaged by austerity. This is particularly so given the land holdings of many local authorities, which can be utilised to support housing development activity. However, income generation is not the only motivating factor. The top desire for authorities engaging in the direct delivery of housing again is simply to deliver housing. There may have been little private sector activity in their area, or insufficient affordable housing or housing for people with particular needs. There may be particular locations needing new housing as part of a broader programme of place-shaping. Local authorities are also strongly motivated to reduce their expenditure on housing those in temporary accommodation and by their duties around homelessness.

There are often a range of motivating factors for local authorities engaging in this area of activity, with a council perhaps being primarily motivated by one aspect but then realising that housing development can assist with other issues as well. There can, however, sometimes be internal conflict about the priority given to each factor and compromises will sometimes need to be agreed: is the aim to maximise affordable housing, generate income or deliver higher-quality housing design? A balance will need to be struck somewhere. Whatever the motivations, a range of powers and sources of funding enable councils to either deliver housing directly from the council itself (through its HRA for socially rented 'council housing' or through its general fund for a slightly wider range of housing) or to establish a wholly owned or joint venture company, which may have a range of objectives but is often more commercially focused on market housing development or property investment or management.

The powers to establish companies under the Localism Act 2011 have been particularly important, as have the abilities to borrow at low interest rates from the PWLB and to utilise the council's own land holdings to develop. In the next chapter, we explore the extent of local authority activity, drawing again on our research on local authority direct delivery of housing and housing and property companies.

FOUR

Overcoming austerity effects through local authority direct action?

Introduction

As discussed in Chapter One, local authorities in the UK and internationally have been faced with budget reductions and austerity. While there have been similar periods of public sector budget cuts in the UK that accompanied the financial downturns in the late 1970s and early 1990s (John, 2014), the application of austerity since 2010 has been a political act designed to transform the way in which local authorities operate and are funded (Borges et al, 2013; Gamble, 2015). As the UK is one of the most centralised states in the Organisation for Economic Co-operation and Development (OECD) (OECD, 2017), local authorities have increasingly been dependent on government funding. This has been directly through the Revenue Support Grant (RSG) paid annually by the government to local authorities and indirectly through grants and specific 'deal' initiatives for housing, transport and other investment, including city deals (Waite et al, 2013; O'Brien and Pike, 2015) and growth deals (Ward, 2019). The approach from 2010 onwards, taken by the coalition and then

Conservative governments, has been more fundamental and revolutionary (Taylor-Gooby, 2012). In 2010, the government decided that the RSG funding paid to councils would be removed and this was implemented through annual tapering to zero by 2020 (Lowndes and Gardner, 2016; LGA, 2018).

It was intended that the RSG would be replaced by each council's retention of 75% of the local business rates. However, this is essentially an inequitable system, as land values vary between different local authorities. Those areas with the greatest need frequently have the lowest land values. It also means that, in practice, councils have to return to a system where they raise revenue for local services through property taxes. This is similar to the system of local government funding that operated until local government reorganisation in 1974, although up to that point, local authorities were provided with funding to build and manage social housing (HMSO, 1981; Chandler, 2013). Some councils also received specific funding for education and social care but as the local authority roles have been reduced, particularly through the introduction of academies into education provision, this has meant that some of the base costs of running a local authority, which were shared between services, now have a much smaller service base to draw on.

As well as the government removing this financial support to individual local authorities, as mentioned in Chapter One, it has remained difficult for councils to increase the level of local council tax, which has remained centrally controlled. However, councils have been able to increase property tax income through allowing more houses to be built in their areas. This approach by councils has been incentivised by the government through the provision of a short-term funding scheme – the New Homes Bonus – which, in effect, make up the shortfall in property tax until the homes are registered onto the system (Sheppard and Smith, 2011; Wilson, 2015). Many councils have become reliant on this source of funding to run their services (Dunning et al, 2014).

Local authorities have been responding to the effects of this centrally imposed austerity through different approaches. Councils initially responded to these funding changes in the same ways as in the past – that is, through a 'salami slicing' approach to their budgets and gradually reducing services (Needham and Mangham, 2014). However, the scale of change after 2010 meant a more fundamental approach was required. Local authorities transferred some services, such as libraries, to communities to maintain their presence (Casselden et al, 2017), while some services, such as many youth and leisure services, were closed altogether (Findlay-King et al, 2018). These cuts have also led to other issues that have costs for society, such as increases in knife crime and the public health effects of closing Sure Start centres for young children (Melhuish et al, 2010). Austerity has recently been linked to a stalling of the usual rises in (and for certain groups, an actual decline in) life expectancy in the UK (Marmot 2020).

The consequences of the persistent and increasing austerity cuts have led to a range of local government responses. Some councils have merged their back-office services or have informal joint working for service delivery. Increasingly, councils are seeking to formally change their status by becoming new and larger councils. There has also been an increase in cross-council service provision. In some cases, councils have sought local solutions through joint working with their local anchor institutions, as in Preston, while in Wigan, there has been a joint approach between the council, public institutions and the community (Thompson et al, 2020). The Public Services (Social Value) Act 2012 has provided more opportunities for local authorities to deliver using value rather than price. Some councils have taken up the approach to wider municipal entrepreneurialism through the provision of traded services such as for the provision of energy, trade waste and housing management. Finally, the majority of local authorities have started to engage in the provision of housing, both to meet their local needs and to generate income. These approaches are discussed in more detail later in this chapter.

This chapter draws on examples of different types of local authority across England and illustrates the ways in which they have been responding to austerity through the use of shared experience and changing institutional structures. As discussed in Chapter Three, there is also growing evidence that local authorities are engaging in the direct provision of housing as one of these responses as a means of re-establishing local government's community credibility, meeting local needs and generating some income to support wider council services, and the extent and means of such activity are explored further in this chapter. We start with responses other than the direct delivery of housing, before drawing on our own research's primary data to illustrate the extent and examples of activity around housing development.

Mergers, combined authorities and joint working

Councils that have been trying to find ways in which they can reduce their back-office costs and overheads have started to develop joint ways of working, which vary between councils. The most minimal form of joint working is where one council delivers a service for another. This can be undertaken through a simple contracting arrangement or through a joint approach to service delivery between two or three councils, using a simple governance approach of a joint committee as set out in Section 101 of the Local Government Act 1972 and where one of the councils either provides the service or manages a contract on behalf of all the councils involved (Tomkinson, 2017). In Rutland, the local plan has been prepared by officers in the neighbouring South Kesteven Council. This is part of a wider Welland Partnership agreement to support five councils working together that was established in 1997. It now includes audit and procurement services, has established a limited liability partnership and a development company.

Some councils undertake procurement, benefits payments or payroll for other councils (Dixon and Elston, 2019).

In 2007, the South Worcestershire Councils Partnership was established by three councils – Worcester City, Malvern Hills and Wychavon – to deliver revenue and benefits services on behalf of all three councils and using a joint committee structure. This has been extended to other services such as information and communications technology (ICT), procurement, planning and building control. The three councils also have a partnership relationship with three more councils for the management of regulatory services across the whole of the Worcestershire County Council area. Some services such as finance and payroll are shared between two of the three South Worcestershire Councils Partnership. This flexible mix-and-match approach is emerging as a more common form of joint working. A range of other examples of planning being delivered as a shared service between councils is provided in Clifford (2018).

Some councils have gone beyond these partnerships for specific service delivery arrangements. In 2016, 46 English councils shared a chief executive and senior management team (LGA, 2016), while others have joined together their back-office staff, such Worthing and Adur on the south coast and Wandsworth and Richmond-upon-Thames in London (Morphet, 2017). Some of these mergers have been tried and found not to have been successful, such as the tri-borough approach in London between Kensington and Chelsea, Hammersmith and Fulham, and Westminster from 2011 to 2017. Here the councils were all within the same political control when the arrangement was established but this was broken when political control changed in one of the boroughs (Carr-West, 2017). Indeed, most partnerships have been between authorities with the same political leadership,

The approach in Worthing and Adur has been operational for nearly 20 years and is based on having joint staff and a joint chief executive while operating the councils separately.

One of the proposals for local government reorganisation in the 1990s joined Worthing and Adur with Brighton and Hove (Stoker, 1997). This was not the selected option, but their joint working appears to have developed as part of these discussions. This approach has now been adopted in London between Wandsworth and Richmond-upon-Thames. In these two councils, Wandsworth is regarded as more politically stable while Richmond-upon-Thames can change political control at each local election every four years. These two local authorities have very different cultures, where Wandsworth has been one of the leading boroughs in London for building housing while Richmond-upon-Thames is the only London borough that seems to be taking no action in providing housing (Morphet and Clifford, 2019). Council partnerships based on known differences might be more resilient than those based on a common political agenda as such agendas may change over time.

Beyond the combined back-office approach, some councils have gone further towards implementing institutional changes between them. In Suffolk, two sets of councils have joined together in a more formal way after periods of joint working. Waveney and Suffolk Coastal and St Edmundsbury and Forest Heath councils have been working together for some years to save resources and have recently merged into two larger councils with the same set of functions (East Suffolk and West Suffolk Councils respectively) (Smulian, 2019). These are all Conservative-controlled councils. West Somerset Council, a small rural council, ran into financial difficulties and was supported by the neighbouring larger Taunton Deane Council in 2019. These two councils (which are both Liberal Democrat controlled) have now merged in the same way as those in Suffolk. Some councils have gone beyond these mergers and have created a larger version of the same type of local authority. In 2019, the nine local authorities in Dorset merged into two new large unitary councils after working together for some time. This was a bottom-up approach. Two councils that had formerly been part of Dorset, Bournemouth and Poole, had already been created as unitary councils in 1997, while the other Dorset councils remained in a two-tier structure with a county council. In 2019, both the unitary and remaining Dorset councils were formally reconstituted into two large unitary councils incorporating the county council within them (the two new authorities are Bournemouth, Christchurch and Poole Council and Dorset Council).

We have also seen the rise of the combined authority, which is a formal grouping of two or more local authorities wishing to pool appropriate responsibilities, often in relation to transport and economic policy. There are currently ten in England. Eight of these are led by a directly elected mayor, which means that a devolution deal has been signed between those authorities and central government to receive certain delegated functions and funding, which can include aspects of transport, housing and social care (Institute for Government, 2019). The access to the funds agreed in the devolution deal and additional powers means combined authorities are potentially attractive to local authorities and seen as a way to counter some of the effects of austerity. Combined authorities were introduced as a concept in the Local Democracy, Economic Development and Construction Act 2009 and later extended in the Cities and Local Government Devolution Act 2016 (Morphet, 2017).

Lowndes and Gardner (2016) highlight the role of the 'Core Cities' group of the eight largest cities in England in lobbying government around the benefits of further devolution and autonomy over economic development in the lead- up to combined authorities, with the Grater Manchester Combined Authority leading the way. In 2015, a devolution deal gave the combined authority strategic oversight of around £7 billion of transferred funding for health, social care and other services on condition of the adoption of a directly elected mayor. Ward et al (2015) argue that the existing strong networks and relationships within and beyond Greater Manchester were fundamental to the Manchester devolution deal being the first and that other local authorities may not be so well placed, economically or politically, to benefit from similar deals, although we have now seen another seven across England. Phelps and Miao (2019) categorise devolution deals and the preceding policy of city deals as a new urban managerialist attempt to avoid having to cut services.

Municipal socialism

One response to austerity that has been adopted in some local authorities is akin to a reversion to the older tradition of municipal socialism (Ward et al, 2015; Thompson, 2020; Thompson et al, 2020). As an approach, it has been developed in the United States, through the Evergreen Cooperatives in Cleveland, Ohio (Howard et al, 2010; Rowe et al, 2017) and based on the Mondragon cooperatives in Spain (Schwartz, 2009; Whyte and Whyte, 2014). This approach has been applied by Preston Council following the council's leader's interest in it (Chakrabortty, 2018). The approach focuses on investment within the local community to create positive and dynamic local economies through arrangements between local authorities and the local anchor institutions – that is, the large public sector organisations present in any locality (Porter, 2010). In Preston, the focus on expenditure between local public bodies has meant a growth from £38 million spent in Preston in 2013 to £111 million in 2017 (Hanna et al, 2018). Similar increases in expenditure have also been made in Lancashire, which have increased employment and the size of the local economy. The approach in Preston is to define a 'common wealth' and use a range of community-scale institutional frameworks, including community land trusts, cooperatives, participatory budgeting and anchor institution procurement. The council is also supporting the creation of cooperatives to establish some business growth (Chakrabortty, 2018), and using this approach to find alternatives to private sector procurement for service delivery (Blakeley, 2019).

Thompson (2020) categorises the approach of Preston as 'managed municipalism'. Preston Council has been Labour controlled for all but three years (1976–79) since it was created in 1973.

While there are advocates of this model, there have been discussions about whether it is protectionist – not least as maintaining expenditure locally is reducing that made elsewhere. Second, the focus on the provision of employment may mean that productivity is lowered and there may be a reduced focus on customers rather than providers. Froud (2018) has argued that while positive as an approach, it is not a silver bullet and will not necessarily work in every location. There are also concerns that many of the initiatives remain the preserve of the white male residents of Preston and have not yet spread to others with different heritages (Chakrabortty, 2018).

Another approach that has been taken to attempt to respond to austerity is through shifting a council's focus to the issues facing local communities rather than national priorities, as in Wigan (another authority under Labour control, which has been the case ever since 1973). Here the council has been developing a 'Wigan Deal' since 2013, which is rooted in health and social care services, with a particular focus on housing for older people. This is also a citizen-led approach, which is described as 'asset-based' working. Here the strengths and assets of the community and local institutions are used to improve outcomes. Wigan Council has led this approach, working closely with the NHS. The council lost 40% of its budget and 20% of its workforce between 2009 and 2019 as part of the adjustment to austerity budgets provided by the government, yet it is a local authority where population growth is related to longevity rather than birth rates or in-migration. The changes in the ways in which public services are working together have focused on working cultures, with staff being given 'permission' to innovate and think differently. There has been place-based integrated working across public services, which has also made a difference (Naylor and

Wellings, 2019). The Wigan Deal is also a direct approach from the council to its citizens, communities and businesses so that they can work together (Wigan, 2019). The council has encouraged local people to register for their own accounts online (that enable them to transact business with the Council) and now has 70,000 MyAccount signups (Jordan, 2019). The council has also transferred assets to the community for its use and management.

We also suggest that local authority peer-to-peer lending might be considered here. Some funding for local authority investment in housing and local energy provision has been provided by peer-to-peer lending between councils (Lowndes and Gardner, 2016). This is where one council will either invest in another council or provide short-term financial liquidity for land and property purchase. Since the financial crisis of 2008, local authorities have not benefited from a discounted early payback scheme for PWLB loans from the Treasury. Instead, they have been saving this cash. In 2016, the National Audit Office published a report, which indicated some concerns about the amount of local authority capital being retained in bank accounts and the potential risk this posed following the collapse of the Icelandic Bank (NAO, 2016). Some councils are now using these funds for their own short-term investment, offering loans to other councils. Warrington Council has started a bank to provide investment to other councils and Nottingham City Council has a development company – Blueprint – which is jointly funded by Aviva's Igloo, a pension fund investment arm. In our survey, we found two council housing companies that were supported by loans from other councils.

Social value

One of the main concerns about austerity has been directed towards the existing level of outsourced services that councils have and the contractual commitments they contain, including for payments and service levels. These contractual relationships cannot be changed without the payment of a penalty, which makes them very inflexible. While relieving councils of some of their service delivery operations, they also require to be contract managed. Further, any organisation can outsource a service but cannot pass on ultimate responsibility for what is delivered indirectly. It is also the case that the UK government has always focused on tender acceptance models that prioritise the lowest price rather than the quality of the service to be delivered (Holt et al, 1995). The opening up of the public sector has evolved since the General Agreement on Tariffs and Trade (GATT) Government Procurement Agreement (GPA) (1980), which liberalised public services to private sector company delivery. For GATT member states, this meant that each state needed to assess the areas where access to the public sector was available and where there was a culture of direct provision. In most countries this varied sector by sector and the GPA required that the least open to competition should be addressed first. In the UK, this was implemented through the introduction of privatisation of the nationalised utilities such as transport, energy and telecommunications (Parker, 2009). For local authorities, which ironically had been expanded through the Local Government Act 1972 structural reforms (implemented in 1974) to create larger local authorities to support direct service provision, the government implemented CCT (Morphet, forthcoming).

Since 2010, the government has taken a more positive view of the quality aspects of tendering, although it has been slow to promote it as a preferred approach. The Public Services (Social Value) Act 2012 sets out how public sector procurement can be undertaken using value rather than the lowest price to award a tender. Whereas this has always been an option in establishing tenders, this Social Value Act now makes it a requirement (Floyd, 2013). Guidance on how to implement the Act together with advice on specifying services and the evaluation of tenders have been prepared and consulted on by the government (DCMS, 2018). Since the Act has been implemented, 42% of councils have found that it reduces inequalities while 82% consider that it improves local economic growth (SEUK, 2019) and there is considered to be capacity for its further development.

For some councils, social value is at the heart of their commercialisation strategies (LGA, 2019a) where it is characterised by the way in which local services are run and in the delivery approaches for local users. In these approaches, social value includes a social, economic or environmental value, which is quantifiable and can be expressed as a monetary outcome. Social value may include more employment, more jobs for disabled people and improved environmental quality. This approach to social value is expected to be more embedded in council decision making rather than one-off approaches that might be achieved through contracting. Financial assessment of social value outcomes is expected to include the social return on investment and will deploy cost–benefit analysis as part of decision making. Taking a more inclusive approach across the council organisation is likely to indicate where the opportunities for investment will be located or where more investment might produce a wider range of beneficial outcomes. In some councils, this approach has gone further, and they have decided to try to make their council self-sufficient through a range of commercial services and managing their own activities differently.

Municipal entrepreneurialism: commercial companies and trading services

Local authorities have also responded to government austerity through the development of 'municipal entrepreneurialism'. This term has traditionally been used to describe activity focused on place regeneration and joint ventures to improve the taxation base of localities, which has had more resonance in the United States than in the UK. However, there is a growing level of local authority commercialisation in the UK, which includes a different approach to service delivery both culturally and practically. Jones and Comfort (2019) quote Scarborough Borough Council, which states that 'the core aims' of its commercial strategy is 'to deliver a financial return which contributes to the Council's spending and investment plans and helps sustain priority outcomes for the Borough's residents'. Much of the commercialisation reported in this study relates to the way in which councils are using their assets, such as property, and working in a more 'business-like' fashion rather than the traditional approach in the United States, which has more of a focus on private sector-led growth.

As introduced in Chapter Three, Sections 1 to 7 of the Localism Act 2011 provided opportunities for local authorities to operate in the same way as private sector companies, returning their focus to types of commercial and social delivery that were more common in the pre-1980 period. This legislation has been used to support a range of activities, including returning to the provision of energy. In some cases, this is described as councils having a commercialisation strategy (Civica/CIPFA, 2016). This approach is also advocated by the Local Government Association (LGA), which advises councils to set a strategy for their commercialisation activities rather than undertaking them in a less integrated way (LGA, 2017a). This advice suggests approaching commercialisation within short-, medium- and long-term objectives set by councils before they embark on their programmes. There is also risk involved and, as some councils have found, establishing a company in order to trade services does not always provide the income expected. Some companies and activities will also require investment such as those councils establishing factories for off-site housing construction. Enterprising Warrington was established in 2017 after an extensive examination of the range of commercial activities already being undertaken in different parts of the council. Oxford has set up a commercial drone service for surveying, land mapping and photography.

Nottingham City Council is establishing a trade waste service. Some councils also take the view that, in common with other outsourced services, commercialisation of their own services can make them too distant from their communities and users.

One of the major growth areas of council entrepreneurialism has been the growth of local energy companies. There are examples in Nottingham, Peterborough and Bristol (Armstrong, 2015; Lacey-Barnacle, 2019), which have been established through community interest societies and community benefit companies. Forest Heath has generated more than £1.3 million through its solar farm, of which a quarter has been put back into delivering council services. Portsmouth City Council decided to abandon its energy company as the cost of investment was considered to be too high. In some cases, councils are providing energy to generate income, but in Islington the council is providing energy as a means of saving money for residents. Aylesbury Vale has opted to seek financial self-sufficiency through a range of property activities that provide income. It also set up its own service company, Vale Services, for citizens, but this was subsequently closed down (*Buckingham and Windsor Advertiser*, 2018). Sevenoaks council is also seeking to be self-supporting (LGA, 2017), while some councils are achieving this through charging strategies. Some council organisations such as Transport for London are establishing consultancies to make available their expertise more widely.

Other councils, however, are going beyond these internal strategies to engage in commercial activities on a wider front, 'developing ventures more redolent of nineteenth-century civic traditions' (Lowndes and Gardner, 2016: 370). Some of these ventures have spun off from services provided by councils, such as Essex County Council's 'Place Services', which is a traded service providing consultancy for environmental assessment, planning, design and management (Clifford, 2018). Some councils have long been involved in the ownership and management of transport facilities such as airports (Humphries,

1999; Ison et al, 2011). Other councils own or have shares in conference centres, including Bournemouth, Birmingham and Harrogate. While some local authorities, such as Woking and Mansfield, have always held property portfolios, there has been a significant increase in property acquisition and management in local government as austerity has continued (Grant Thornton, 2018). Twenty-four per cent of local authorities have spun-out employee-owned mutual companies, according to the Localis (2016, in Phelps and Miao, 2019) survey, which found that 58% of councils owned trading companies, following the Local Government Act 2003, and externally traded services generated profits of £1.5 billion for UK local government from 2008 to 2013.

Some companies have used their own property companies to acquire assets in their own areas such as shopping centres or offices, while others have purchased assets elsewhere (Christophers, 2019; Sandford, 2019a ; NAO, 2020). Davies (2018) reports examples of the ways that councils across England have borrowed substantially – in some cases ten times their annual budgets – to finance the purchase of real estate, involving PWLB loans. In 2017–18, authorities spent a total of £1.8 billion on investment properties, a six-fold increase since 2013–14. Spelthorne Council, in Surrey, is highlighted by Davies (2018) as having borrowed £1 billion in total, including for the purchase of a business park in Spelthorne for £392 million. Examples of investments from a range of councils, including properties within and outwith their council areas, are given. Davies (2018) expresses concerns about the accountability of this, and the level of risk authorities are potentially exposed to if property prices/rents fall in future.

Purves (2018) also investigates local authority property investment activity, noting that the former leader of East Hampshire District Council presented a three-pronged strategy to respond to austerity: efficiencies (within the council), sales (providing services to other authorities, the private sector and the public) and investments (income from property). There appears to have been a deliberate move away from selling off assets to instead utilising existing assets, and purchasing further land and property, to generate income. Examining the annual accounts of the district and county councils in Surrey, Purves (2018) finds that borrowing from the PWLB for investment had increased from £15 million in 2004 to £2.5 billion by 2018. He takes a more positive stance than Davies (2018), suggesting that the risks have been overstated, for example that a PWLB loan is not subject to the loan-to-value covenant that would be imposed on a commercial mortgage so that a fall in the value of the asset would not subject the loan to additional security or force a fire sale. He also highlights that the Crown Estate provides a model of how property investment has long been done successfully within the public sector and that some local authorities have utilised investment within property within their own areas to successfully aid regeneration and place-shaping objectives. Purves (2018) considers this activity a form of bringing activity previously carried out by private enterprise into the field of public service, with authorities borrowing money to establish public ownership of land and using the spread between borrowing rates and yields from rental incomes to generate profit to fund public services, which can be considered positively.

This commercial property investment activity has, however, caused concern on the part of central government and this has led to a National Audit Office review of councils investing in commercial property assets (NAO, 2020). This has possibly been stimulated by the property sector lobby, who are regarding local authorities as a disruptive influence in an otherwise stable market. There have been concerns expressed by Members of Parliament (MPs) that local authorities can obtain finance at below market rates from the PWLB and use this to undercut the private sector investor. Another fear has been that local authorities may be bidding against each other, thus increasing the price paid, or that they are inexperienced in their acquisitions and may be paying too much for an asset. Finally, there are concerns where councils may be buying commercial assets within their own town centres, which would otherwise not attract investment.

Faced with this external pressure, the government brought in new financial rules for local authorities in April 2018 to encourage a more cautious approach and to require all councils to prepare an asset investment strategy. The consultation published by central government before the new rules were brought in commented that:

> We do not want to restrict opportunities for local authorities to use commercial structures to kick start local economic regeneration to deliver services more effectively. However, the prime duty of a local authority is to provide services to local residents, not to take on disproportionate levels of financial risk by undertaking speculative investments, especially where that is funded by additional borrowing. (MHCLG, 2018b)

At the same time, the Chartered Institute of Public Finance and Accountancy (CIPFA) – the professional organisation for local authority accountants – is steering local authorities to invest in housing rather than commercial or retail properties (CIPFA, 2019). It is also worth noting that a report from CBRE (2017, in Purves, 2018) estimated that austerity had led to a shortfall in funding for local authorities of £10 billion, but that if all of that were to be sourced from 'geared investment' in property then local authorities would need to invest more than £150 billion in commercial real estate, more than the maximum headroom for all PWLB loans.

The commercial property activity of local authorities may be conducted directly by the local authority or through a wholly owned company. The trading of council services and expertise may be through a trading fund of the council, a wholly owned company trading openly, or a Teckal (a separate entity, which may have a contractual arrangement with a local authority that controls it and which performs at least 80% of its activities on behalf of the local authority, thus not needing to go through public procurement tendering processes). A defining feature of contemporary municipal entrepreneurialism in England (and beyond) is its diversity. The form and modes of control of companies vary considerably: some council companies are established to provide services or functions on behalf of the council – which Ferry et al (2018) term 'corporatisation' – while others are there to generate income for new areas of activity.

Ferry et al (2018) examined local authority annual accounts from 2010/11 to 2016/17 and found an increase from around 400 local authority companies in 2010/11 to about 600 by 2016/17, with the dominant form being companies limited by shares (where the profits can then be reinvested in services by the local authority). Skelcher (2017) found that more than 500 companies had been created by the 150 largest local authorities in England from 2011 to 2017, operating in such areas as social care, museums, housing, educational support, infrastructure and economic development. Skelcher (2017) examined how Birmingham City Council created companies related to IT, property, educational support and museums between 2006 and 2012 but these varied from a joint venture company limited by shares with Capita (for IT), to a wholly owned company limited by shares (for property management and building control services), to wholly owned companies limited by guarantee and with charitable status (for educational support and museums). The companies had been established for a variety of purposes, from a stated desire to improved customer service to reducing employment costs and income generation, including through seeking new trading opportunities. The companies limited by shares were intended to make a profit for distribution elsewhere in the council, whereas the companies limited by guarantee were just to self-fund the service concerned (with considerable tax advantages), which were seen as social goods to be sustained on a not-for-profit basis rather than commercialised. This diversity of objective and form can also be seen in relation to housing companies, which we consider in more detail in the next section. Examples of municipal entrepreneurial activity exist from councils controlled by each of the three main political parties and those with no overall control.

Municipal entrepreneurialism: housing development and companies

Local authorities have traditionally been housing providers but, as discussed in Chapter Two, this role has been stripped away by government both through removing subsidy from councils to support the development of social housing and through the erosion of the housing stock through the introduction of RTB initiatives. While some councils have been providing new housing, councils like Nottingham are losing one home a day from their council stock through RTB. Some 40% of this housing has transferred to the private rented sector, with councils then having to rent back these properties in order to house homeless people (Copley, 2019; Savage, 2019). As discussed in Chapter Three, there are a range of motivations for local authorities to become engaged again in the direct delivery of housing, and a range of means through which they can do this.

Sixty-nine per cent of authorities responding to our survey in 2018 reported that they were engaged directly in the delivery of housing as an authority, an increase on the 65% who reported this in 2017. Of those not engaged, a majority were considering it, leaving just 11% of authorities who were apparently not engaged in nor actively considering engaging in direct housing provision. This engagement can include building social housing through the HRA, building a mix of tenures through the general fund, building through a wholly owned company or building through a joint venture company.

Looking at the regional distribution of local authorities within each category of directly engaged in housing delivery, considering engaging, and not engaging nor considering, the responses to our 2018 survey show that authorities in the East of England, London and the South East are slightly more likely to be engaged in delivery than might be expected from the distribution of authorities across the regions, while those in the East Midlands and North West are less likely to be engaged or considering engaging. This reflects our findings from the 2017 survey. The regional pattern of local authorities with a wholly owned or joint venture housing company reflects this as well. Looking at political control, we can see that Conservative authorities are also slightly less represented than might be expected from the overall distribution within both our survey responses. And, all authorities in England in the group directly delivering housing and authorities not engaged nor considering engaging are significantly more likely to be Conservative than Labour controlled. This again reflects our findings from the 2017 survey. It also reflects the trend with the political control of the more specific set of authorities that have a local housing company. Authorities with a housing company also tend to be more urbanised, with higher housing demand, but there are examples of authorities engaged in housing delivery of all types (district, borough, county, unitary), of all population sizes within the range of English authorities, of all main types of political control and located in all regions.

Our survey of authorities in 2018 found 42% reporting that they had a local housing company, which is similar to the 44% in response to our 2017 survey. In 2018, an additional question was asked about whether the company was wholly owned by the local authority or a joint venture, and 83% of local authorities with a company had a wholly owned housing company, while 34% of local authorities with a company had a joint venture housing company (the overlap is because 7% of local authorities reported that they had both joint venture and wholly owned companies). Hackett (2017) reported that there were about 150 local housing companies across England in 2017 and likely to be around 200 by 2020. He found that they offered councils a 'triple dividend' in the form of delivering extra housing, a greater chance to be actively place-shaping and a financial return to the council.

Our desk surveys of online and public information about every local authority in England in 2017 and 2019 found that 78% had a housing or property company in 2019, with 119 new companies registered between the surveys. There were also 16 companies that appeared to have closed between 2017 and 2019. Some companies may also be dormant, having been registered but not yet doing anything directly (some may then go on to be active, others may never be). The boundaries between property companies (primarily to acquire and manage commercial assets to generate income to support council services) and housing companies (primarily to acquire or build new housing, for a range of motivations) can sometimes be blurred. Most pure property companies do not include housing within their portfolio, but there are companies that are there to manage rather than build housing and companies more focused on acquiring existing housing stock compared with others that are more about building new housing. Councils with a property investment company may also have access to development and professional property skills, which could be extended in future, hence their inclusion.

Looking across this wider range of companies, 57% of authorities appeared to have at least one joint venture. These can vary between who the partners are (sometimes it is another public sector organisation like another council, a housing association or university working with the council, but often a private developer) and the split between the two partners. In many cases, the council has contributed the land and the partner has contributed funding and expertise. While joint ventures have been a popular mechanism for providing housing, with some councils finding them to be useful, particularly where there was a perception of low skill levels within the council, there were several other opinions raised during our research. Some councils found that working with joint venture partners was slower than if they were developing through their own company. Some councils considered that the arrangements for the use of technical expertise and advice did not work well. Others were concerned about the financial arrangements and levels of profit being made by the private sector joint venture partner. Overall, the main concerns about council joint ventures were about the speed of development and the inability of the local authority to influence their joint venture partner in this. There were also concerns about the type of development being provided and whether or not it was likely to be policy compliant in its delivery.

Whatever the precise numbers, there has clearly been a remarkable growth of local authority direct engagement in housing delivery over the past decade, and a considerable number of local housing companies established since the Localism Act 2011. Through their naming, the companies may be obviously linked to a council, such as Eastbourne Council's Eastbourne Housing Investment Company Ltd, or not, such as South Norfolk Council's Big Sky Group (an umbrella organisation of three companies established by a Conservative-controlled council). Sometimes the naming is linked to the purpose of the company or perceptions around building 'council housing' and whether the housing would sell (if the company is building market-sale housing). Company directors are usually a mixture of council officers and elected councillors and companies are usually staffed by a mixture of council staff and consultants (Hackett, 2017).

Most local authorities have just one company, but some authorities have more, often established for different purposes. For example, Eastleigh Council has four such companies: Aspect Building Communities Ltd, established in December 2014; Spurwing Developments Ltd, established in March 2016 but apparently voluntarily wound up in February 2020; Spurwing Ventures Ltd, established in November 2016 but apparently voluntarily wound up in February 2020; and Pembers LLP, established in September 2017 as a joint venture with Galliford Try. Exeter also reported, in response to our survey, four companies but noted that three were dormant and only one was currently active.

Oxford Council reported five companies: Oxford City Housing Ltd (a parent or holding company established for the buying and selling of its own real estate and operation of leased real estate, established in June 2016); Oxford City Housing (Investment) Ltd (primarily focused on social rented housing, procuring the anticipated 354 social rented housing units being delivered at the new mixed-tenure development at Barton Park under a Section 106 agreement); Oxford City Housing (Development) Ltd (aiming to develop mixed-tenure housing, selling the affordable housing to the city council and with an approved development pipeline of 215 homes, 50% of which will be affordable); Barton Oxford LLP (a joint venture with Grosvenor Developments established in September 2011 and which apparently made a loss of £1.7 million in 2019, albeit with £20 million worth of assets in relation to the ongoing development of Barton Park, a scheme to develop 885 new homes on a 94-acre greenfield site owned by the city council); and Barton Park Estate Management Company Ltd (a dormant company established in August 2016, which seems to be ready as an estate management company for when the development at Barton Park is complete, with directors from both the city council and Grosvenor Developments) (Hays, no date; Companies House, 2020).

Considering examples of local authority activity from our research illustrates the multitude of approaches local authorities have taken to engaging in the direct delivery of housing again, and the multitude of rationales and motivations such activity responds to. First and foremost, there is a clear desire among local authorities to see affordable housing delivered and to respond to local housing need through their own activity. This is often typified by larger authorities, particularly (but not exclusively) those under Labour control, building through their HRA again. Bristol City Council owns 40% of all land in its area, and 15% of all housing. Between 2015 and 2019, it had built 101 new council homes. The development of new homes using the HRA is guided by the need to reduce costs and make use of all of the sites that the council owns, with a focus on derelict sites that can be brought back into use. The council is also focusing on improving areas for local communities, addressing the demand for affordable housing in Bristol and helping reduce antisocial behaviour on derelict sites. The council has started the next phase of the new-build council housing programme and is developing 11 sites over the next three years, which it aims will provide around 550 new homes.

In London, Southwark Council has developed a 30-year HRA business plan. A manifesto commitment from the ruling Labour Group was to deliver 1,500 homes by the end of 2018, for social rent. It is then aiming to deliver 11,000 homes by 2043. This includes developing out council-owned surplus sites and looking for 'hidden homes' opportunities. It has worked with a community land trust in partnership with housing associations on two sites on council-owned land, to deliver 400 units. Southwark is buying properties from the affordable housing contributions under Section 106 agreements. In all approaches, it is seeking to develop at high quality. It registered a company in 2015, when this became popular among London boroughs. It had been considering the potential role for its housing company in delivering housing for key workers and was concerned about the low amount of intermediate rent provision in the borough, so it thought there may be a role for the company in helping to address that as well. However, it seems that the government lifting the HRA debt cap meant that attention was focused on building directly through that rather than through the company, which has remained dormant.

Camden Council has a major programme to deliver 3,050 homes directly through a community investment programme using the HRA. The council has also set up Camden Living, a council-owned provider of affordable rented homes, with many set at a Camden living rent and available to households with incomes between £30,000 and £40,000, with any surplus made contributing to the council's service delivery. The council has considered development for market sale, but this is perceived to be riskier in a changing market and the council is turning to providing private rented housing on small sites. The removal of the HRA debt cap has supported the council in providing more housing, as has the Mayor of London's skills fund to help build up housing development skills internally and with Islington and Hackney.

Islington Council likewise is working proactively to deliver more council housing through the HRA, receiving the support of £24.2 million in 2018 from the Mayor of London's provision for new council housing. The delivery of new housing, particularly affordable housing, is a high political priority in Islington. Local councillors are very ambitious. The council has a team of 18 staff in its 'new build' team for the direct delivery of housing and has recently appointed a new service director specifically responsible for new-build activity. The council aims to deliver 1,900 genuinely affordable homes between 2018 and 2022, of which 550 will be for council homes for social rent and the rest will be for the private market in mixed-tenure schemes. Islington is not using a company. There was some reluctance about joint ventures given some other council experiences, and, while the council has set up a wholly owned company for other purposes, the lifting of the HRA debt cap has made the use of this wholly owned company to deliver new homes a less attractive proposition. Rather, the council is directly delivering these new homes, which it believes is the best model. It wants to maximise the delivery of social housing and needs some private market housing to cross-subsidise this. It is not looking to make a profit for the council from these private homes, however, but rather to maximise affordable housing delivery so that any money made from the private units goes straight to funding more social units.

The new affordable homes are funded both through the cross-subsidy from the private market homes, but also through HRA borrowing, a Greater London Authority grant and RTB receipts. The central government–imposed rent cut did, however, wipe £1 billion off the value of the Islington HRA, hence a higher proportion of the new build had to go to private sales than originally anticipated (when there would have been much more social rent), although the broad aim remains 70:30 for affordable to market now the council is able to borrow. There is a strong emphasis on design quality, as it wants high-quality homes both for its own portfolio of council housing but also for income from the private market to subsidise that. Furthermore, as most sites are on existing estates, it is looking to deliver broader public realm improvements through its own new-build developments so that existing residents see a benefit too (for example improvements to estate open space and play space, including greening). The emphasis on high-design quality has evolved over ten years and includes both internal and external design. The council goes for high-quality materials for the homes and the communal areas/public realm. There is a desire to future-proof developments, with consideration of electric car charging, green roofs and energy efficiency. Space standards are achieved. The council also gets contractors to try to do more to resolve snagging and to do a proper handover to new residents.

The new-build programme developed quite organically but it has now built out 30 schemes over ten years and gone from 15 to almost 200 homes of all tenure per annum. This requires an expanding team of staff, and careful work on finances. The process is completely in-house, from feasibility work to handover. Skills can be a challenge, particularly around project management, and particularly given most London boroughs now have a new-build programme. At present, private developers, housing associations and boroughs are all in competition for the same pool of people. Internal upskilling work is thus vital. External commercial sales teams are currently used for the council's private market new builds; however, people seem to trust the service they get from the council as a local authority (feeling there is better accountability) and Hackney Council has an in-house sales team for private units, which Islington council may access in the future.

The 550 new council homes will all be built on council-owned sites. The council has looked at acquiring sites, but it is hard to compete with private developers and housing associations for these. It has, however, worked with the Greater London Authority on fire and police service surplus sites, as well as successfully purchasing a site from the NHS. After meeting the 2022 target for new-build units, the council would like to deliver more than the 550 affordable units for 2018–22, but to be realistic, and to continue to be a beacon for good quality. The council's own new-build developments go through the same open book viability process as a private development. The affordable housing contributions can be an issue regarding the viability of a scheme versus the council's objective to provide very high percentages of affordable housing. There are some negotiations over the contributions to the public realm and community facilities.

Smaller authorities, of various political control, are also demonstrating that it is possible to build directly under the HRA again. For example, the former Taunton Deane Council (now merged with West Somerset) has had an active HRA, did not consider that there is a need to establish a housing company and has developed approximately 50 homes each year since 2012. Babergh and Mid-Suffolk are two neighbouring district councils (both with currently no overall political control) that now have one integrated body of staff. They are using their HRA capital and RTB receipts to fund new builds, delivering 65 units between 2015 and 2018. The strategy is then a further 300 homes between 2018 and 2021. These homes are built in partnership with a local development partner who has skills around architecture, planning and cost consultancy. They have just acquired four sites from the county council and will deliver about 25 sites on each. They have used a geographic information system (GIS) to identify potential surplus district council land that could be used for housing development, with local planners assisting with the policy screening of these sites. Hartlepool Council, meanwhile, has been purchasing properties with Section 106 monies and looking to manage them directly, hence it became the first authority in 21st-century England to reopen an HRA, having previously transferred its stock. There are now 280 properties under its HRA. As well as old terraced houses needing refurbishment, the council is also buying new builds on private development sites and purchasing former Council housing sold under RTBs as well to help diversify the portfolio of property it holds.

Ensuring housing delivery that meets the needs of all residents is something else driving local authorities. There are also some councils that are specialising in providing housing for people with particular needs. In some local authorities, like Wigan in Greater Manchester, the foreseeable population growth in their area will be derived from longevity rather than birth or in-migration. If people are going to be living longer then it is important to keep them warm, healthy and active. Many homeowners with lower-valued properties cannot afford to insulate their homes and are not eligible for grant aid from the local authority. Yet the need to retrofit homes to meet fuel poverty and the climate crisis increases yearly (Smith Institute, 2018). However, unless local authorities develop their own housing to meet people's needs, which can include housing for families, disabled people, key workers as well as older people, they cannot reserve land for this purpose in their local plans until other providers emerge.

Eastbourne Council (currently Liberal Democrat controlled) has directly delivered housing, acting as developer, through its HRA. It has delivered 100 units and has acquired and refurbished existing properties to help with neighbourhood regeneration. It has one of the first local authority companies, the Eastbourne Housing Investment Company, founded in

May 2015. It is wholly owned by the council and received some working capital from the general fund to help establish it. The strategic objectives are income generation, place-shaping and meeting strategic housing targets. The private sector housing market locally has been described as 'dysfunctional', not delivering enough affordable housing and particularly not delivering enough for older people, despite the make-up of the local population. There has therefore been a drive around ensuring housing fit for older people, with things like the Lifetime Homes standard, is being delivered. The company was named the 'new developer of the year' in the 2016 UK Housing Awards. Profits in 2019 were around £900,000 (Companies House, 2020).

Alongside providing housing for older people, there has also been a concern around design quality. Norwich City Council (currently Labour controlled) is using its own new-build programme under its HRA to not only deliver new housing but also to invest in skills training and demonstrate the opportunity of Passivhaus construction. Homes are developed to a high specification (for example in terms of space standards and energy efficiency – reducing costs for residents and maintenance bills for the council). A hundred and five homes on Goldsmith Street were funded by funded by a mix of borrowing, council reserves and RTB receipts and won the RIBA Stirling Prize in 2019 (Wainwright, 2019 a, b).

As well as a concern with the design of individual housing, there can also be a broader concern with place-shaping and the ability to use the council's own direct delivery of housing in relation to place-shaping agendas. For example, Wolverhampton Council has been keen to extend the range of housing on offer in its area. The council has an active arm's-length management organisation with 2,200 homes and that is building 400–500 properties in two areas and has 200 homes in the pipeline. The council's company, WV Living, plans to build 1,200 homes in four to five years, starting on a site for homes for market sale for first-time buyers, together with affordable, starter and market rent homes on the same site. The council is delivering more housing to deal with derelict sites and to support the economic regeneration of the city centre.

In Tower Hamlets and Birmingham, the local authorities have expanded their existing HRA teams and started to build across a range of tenures that meet local need not met by the private sector. This has included traditional council social rented housing for older people and young graduates in Birmingham and for homeless people in Tower Hamlets. In Nottingham, the council is also intervening to meet different objectives. It is creating a new market of housing for sale to kick-start regeneration while also making efforts to meet climate and fuel poverty issues on its own council stock, using a Dutch *Energiesprong* method and funded by the European Union (EU) (Vaughan, 2019). This is a combination approach of cladding and solar energy panels for existing council housing that reduces energy costs significantly. The council is also, like other cities such as Leeds and Durham, using its land and property powers to maintain tenure mix in areas that might otherwise be fully taken over by students (Jones, 2018).

Some councils have always undertaken housing and property development to supplement their incomes through the acquisition of commercial properties and this emerging approach across the majority of local authorities is an extension of this. In some areas, this market rented stock is also provided by councils to meet other objectives in addition to income by providing higher-quality market rent accommodation to retain graduates in their areas. In councils that have a university, students frequently leave the area after graduating as the rental market properties are not as new as those provided through student accommodation. In providing rented accommodation for young graduates, councils such as Stoke-on-Trent and Birmingham find that this encourages them to remain in their university town. Some councils, such as Middlesbrough, have also found that graduates are taking over commercially provided housing that was intended for students. Some councils, such as Bristol, are providing mixed tenures so that market sale and rents can offset and cross-subsidise social and affordable rented homes within these developments. However, councils are also critical of the ways in which student accommodation financial models work in the private sector, with fragmented 'pods' appealing to small investors who can purchase with a smaller outlay and start earning income very quickly. Alongside concerns about the guaranteed returns promised on these investments (Lunn, 2019), this type of investment makes prices higher for suitable sites and can price out other types of housing development.

Where local authorities still maintain their existing stock, some councils have considered optimising their land and type of development through the redevelopment of housing for sale. In some councils, there have been major joint ventures with the private sector to deliver this type of development. However, some of these have been marked by controversy and there appears to be a bit of a shift, with the approaches now being adopted by councils more focused on providing housing to meet local housing need, particularly homelessness, which bears both a financial and a social cost. The changes in benefit rules and the Local Housing Allowance have made it difficult for many people, including those families in work, to combat the practices of private landlords, who may prefer to re-let their properties at higher rent values. The increasing difficulties of many young people to purchase their own home, with the government's First Homes scheme failing to deliver, has increased pressure on the private rental market.

Income generation to offset austerity is, of course, a key motivator for local authorities in engaging in the direct delivery of housing again, particularly those doing this through a company. County Durham's wholly owned company, Chapter Homes, directly delivers new homes. The company owns housing as well as commercial property and related activity. It has delivered 800 units so far. At present its primary aim is income generation for the local authority, but there are potentially shifting priorities, and some local politicians apparently seem to have a belief that the company can do everything. Chapter Homes aims for 14% profit (compared with about 22% for private housebuilders), with the slightly lower margin due to building to better quality, including good design and space standards. There is a ten-year business plan and pipeline of sites for Chapter Homes, developing on council-owned sites. Other local authorities have been interested in learning from Durham, but a lot depends on the individual circumstances of each authority, for example landownership.

There has also been discussion as to whether income generation should be reduced in order to concentrate on providing housing that might help towards the unmet local demand for elderly, supported and social housing, but there is an active need to have a balance between generating income (to support council services) and having a more social focus. The branding as 'Chapter Homes' was deliberate as it was felt this would be more attractive to the private market than just being explicitly 'the council'; however, it seems that people are reassured that it is the council behind it as there seems a higher level of trust than with some private developers. Skills apparently remain a key challenge. Staff often move around between private developers and registered providers. Development surveyor skills present a particular challenge, as well as skills in asset management and in legal, as to do new-build development as a local authority, there is a need to resource the staff to support the entire development journey. The company appears to be successful, with the 2019 accounts showing £3.7 million in net assets (Companies House, 2020).

Derbyshire Development Limited was a company wholly owned by Derbyshire County Council. Its prime objective was around income generation, following concern that county council sites were being sold to private developers who were making a profit from them, which the council was not sharing in. There were a range of other objectives, such as employment and skills (for example construction apprenticeships for local youth, particularly those out of care) and housing delivery, but making up for the loss of the RSG was paramount. The aim was for a small company that would primarily buy in the expertise it needs (for example around planning, development and construction) from external consultants, starting with two sites and aiming to actually deliver housing rather than land banking, benefiting both the district councils (which have housing need) and the county council (which needs to generate income). Filings at Companies House appear to show that the company has, however, ceased trading, demonstrating the challenges around starting up housing development on a much more commercial basis.

Other authorities are explicitly using a mixture of means and responding to a mixture of motivations for housing development. Sometimes there can be tensions evident. In East Devon, the council has an HRA and a company. The council used its HRA to play an enabling role and it has also had considerable RTB receipts to spend quickly, which it has used to purchase properties in the open market. While the council is keen to build, it does not have much land in its HRA. There have been some tensions within the council between planning and the company and there has also been competition with registered providers to acquire market housing sites. Swindon also has an HRA and a company. The HRA has been building bungalows and housing for people with particular needs, completing about 50 homes per year over the past five years. The council's housing company is focused on providing income and develops the smaller sites available to it.

Slough is another council using multiple means to deliver housing. It has built directly under the HRA and also purchased properties, which have then come into its HRA. From 2005 to 2011, the council built about 120 houses to respond to family needs, using redundant sites on existing estates (a 'garage strategy'). Originally, the council would develop properties but then sell them to registered social landlords to manage, whereas now the council manages properties directly. It is still building homes directly under its HRA on council-owned small sites, tendering out the actual building work.

The council has also utilised companies, including joint venture and wholly owned companies. There are four companies: Development Initiative for Slough Housing – DISH – established in January 1988; Slough Urban Renewal LLP, founded in October 2012 as a joint venture between Slough Borough Council and another company called 'Community Solutions for Regeneration (Slough) Ltd', which in turn is wholly owned by Morgan Sindall (showing the complexity of disentangling some of these relationships) and which, according to Companies House filings, made a £7 million profit in 2017; James Elliman Homes Ltd, founded in February 2017; and Herschel Homes, founded in February 2017 but currently dormant (Companies House, 2020).

The joint venture with Morgan Sindall redevelops council-owned land for housing, as well as commercial and community buildings. The affordable housing developed through this becomes council owned. There is also a council wholly owned company, James Elliman Homes. It has leased properties for temporary housing needs and is currently looking at ways to develop key worker housing. Section 106 agreements on private development sites include an affordable housing contribution as the top priority. In the past, this would go to registered social landlords but now some are going directly to the council's company, which sees this as good value. These are on smaller sites, which registered social landlords do not seem interested in. When the council is the developer, there is apparently a need to work internally to manage expectations. Different parts of the authority can have different expectations, for example around design quality compared with income generation concerns.

Bournemouth Council is another authority taking a varied approach. Bournemouth has an in-house development team with a project manager, project officer and surveying team. The council was keen to develop housing again as soon as possible in 2009 and has delivered about 200 units directly through the HRA and the general fund. A quarterly gathering of key staff looks at all council-owned surplus sites to consider if they can be used for housing. They feel they can deliver more affordable units, and that the council's own development activity has helped to stimulate more private sector development in the town. An active apprenticeship programme is also operating. The council also has four different local authority owned companies. Bournemouth Development Company Ltd is developing out 20 surface car parks (being replaced with multi-storey provision with housing on top) and has built out three sites already, primarily as private rented sector housing. The Bournemouth Building Maintenance Company was founded after the private maintenance contractor for the retained housing stock went bankrupt, and has taken on the vital work while generating profit for the general fund. Seascape South is a commercial construction company owned by the council. Seascape Homes and Property, meanwhile, acquires existing property and uses is to tackle homelessness, with 50 units purchased so far. It is currently investigating sites for further housing development potential, as well as considering the potential of new construction techniques (such as modular housing) for smaller sites.

Finally, Birmingham City Council is often considered an exemplar authority for successfully engaging in housing delivery again. It is delivering new homes for rent, for sale and for the private rented sector, primarily doing this directly under its HRA and general fund under the branding of 'Birmingham Municipal Housing Trust'. The council is Britain's largest council landlord, with 61,000 homes, and has built more than 3,000 homes from inception in 2009, with more than 300 under construction, making it the country's biggest local authority housebuilder (Barker, 2019). It was inspired into action by the large housing waiting list and numbers in temporary accommodation and decline in private sector new-home completions in the city after the financial crash. The HRA subsidy reform made it viable for the council to start building council housing again, for the first time since the 1970s, and drawing also on Homes and Community Agency/Homes England grant funding in the same way as a housing association.

More than 1,000 new social/affordable rent homes were completed between 2009 and 2017, all on council-owned sites and within the HRA. It has also looked at unmet demand for bungalows, which the private sector was not delivering, and designed the 'Birmingham Dormer Bungalow', a bespoke design delivered with good space standards, Code 4 for sustainable homes and Lifetime Homes standards. It also developed more than 1,000 homes for sale in partnership with private developers between 2009 and 2017, with council architects doing the design and planners securing the planning permission. The council receives a guaranteed plot value and share of any overage, which is then used to help fund the construction of homes for social rent. It has also been keen to improve the standards of design and management of the private rented sector in the city and so has developed some apartment schemes on site deemed more suitable for this than for social rent or sale.

Birmingham Council now builds over 25% of all new housing in the city. When presenting on this activity, the council argues that the construction-related activity benefits the city's economy and local businesses, that the council can exercise control to improve standards of design and build quality, and that it maximises economic benefits for the city by following the Birmingham Business Charter for Social Responsibility (Birmingham City Council, 2020). Benefits are seen to include increased council tax revenues and local jobs and apprenticeships. Council officers present this activity as 'socially responsible capitalism' and an example of 'municipal enterprise' in the tradition of Victorian-era mayor Joseph Chamberlain (Skidmore, 2017).

In general, looking across the local authority experience, land is often a central concern. In providing housing, 95%

councils have been using their own land and the identification of council-owned land has offered more opportunities for development than previously understood. While councils can own considerable amounts of land, only a few sites may have been identified as suitable for housing. However, with initiatives such as One Public Estate (Sandford, 2019b), which have supported mapping all public sector landownership on a GIS base, it has been easier for local authority staff to take a more in-depth examination of the sites that might be available. Even small sites might be suitable for the custom-build registers that councils are required to maintain. In the past, councils might traditionally have sold land for development to the commercial sector or undertaken a joint venture with them or a housing association. However, increasingly councils are retaining and developing it directly. In some councils, development is taking place on golf courses or former surface-level car parks. Some councils are releasing commercial space from town centres to introduce housing to support their economies. The development of these sites is not always easy. The design and construction of small sites can be challenging (LB Croydon, 2018) and the costs higher than on larger schemes, although some councils are packaging smaller and larger sites together to reduce the costs of single developments. Servicing and parking are also more difficult on smaller sites, but small sites are frequently completed more rapidly than larger sites that offer higher numbers of homes overall. In rural areas, small sites can be important for affordable provision in villages.

Those councils that are at the forefront of direct delivery are often adopting some practices that are making them more successful. In particular, councils establishing single housing delivery teams across all their housing activities – including planning, development, partnerships and homelessness – appear to be making more progress. These teams, of mixed professionals including planning, transport and housing officers, together with finance, legal and development surveyors, are increasing their knowledge of development costs, intervening to meet bridging loans where there may be infrastructure issues that need to be resolved as part of development and taking a proactive approach to all housing sites. In some councils, a customer relations management type system is being used that associates all actions in relation to any site in one place and makes one officer the lead for that site. This officer will also be the single point of contact on any individual site. These sites are actively and continuously reviewed. When developers suggest that there may be problems in bringing forward development, the council has all the necessary information available about the site and about the local market and construction conditions with which to assess the developer's claims. These councils also frequently have a housing delivery board chaired by a leading politician, which meets very regularly to review the housing sites and progress of development schemes. They are also likely to have a housing development forum that all those involved in housing delivery and management are expected to attend, including charities, developers, housing associations and landowners. These whole-council approaches may be challenging to establish, given other departmental and political priorities, but they are proving to be effective in housing delivery across all types of housing.

Conclusions

The approaches of councils to providing services to offset cuts and austerity, discussed in this chapter, can be regarded as an effort of functional statecraft within a broader frame of municipal statecraft (Lauermann, 2018). The approaches to local authority intervention in the market have generally been directed towards market failure and this is the case with some of the current approaches, particularly in relation to social care and meeting some types of housing need. However, the approaches identified here, some of which are now being used across the majority of English local authorities, are about another kind of action and that is for financial security. The effects of austerity have caused local authorities to rethink their models of action. This has not resulted in a removal or reduction of all services, in a 'small state' approach favoured by Chancellor George Osborne in 2010, but rather a mechanism to put local government on a different and more independent financial footing, which enables them to meet social needs. The evidence here is strong across all types of councils and all parts of the country. While some approaches have been more favoured by some political controls than others (for example more municipal socialist approaches are associated with Labour-controlled authorities), there are examples of most of the approaches we have discussed in this chapter from councils of all different political majorities. As Lauermann (2016) sets out, councils are now establishing diversified approaches to investment, both short and long term, and also have a range of broader objectives as noted in the councils providing housing. The use of cross-subsidy, which will use housing for sale to provide housing for social rent, is now commonplace. Councils are also establishing property portfolios that will provide long-arm income in the same ways as patient investors in the property sector. Councils are now less likely to just sell their land but instead either develop it directly or maintain an interest in it if developed by others.

These approaches have also included innovation and experimentation. As the example of the Wigan Deal demonstrates, there is a new approach that seeks a joint set of commitments and actions across the local authority rather than supporting a dependency culture with an expectation that the state will provide all. The approach in Preston is also one that is self-supporting and where the council has already built 900 new homes with its private sector partner Hive. These councils are dependent on the quality and vision of their own leadership to innovate and extend these approaches into the future. The councils that are implementing structural reforms are taking a different approach. For some this is based on cooperating but for others this longer-term relationship has been put into new local government frameworks so that there will be commitment to maintain these relationships over time. This all has implications for central–local relations. There are also potential risks, as well as benefits, and broader questions for the future of local government and the publics it serves. We turn to consider these in our next, concluding, chapter.

FIVE

Austerity's legacy: risk, opportunity and a new form of central–local relations?

Introduction

As discussed in Chapter One, local authorities in England have been faced with the twin crises of managing housing demand and supply and responding to super-austerity. Severe budget cuts have occurred in authorities in England, and many other places internationally. As this book has demonstrated, local authorities in England have taken a range of initiatives to respond to austerity. These have been institutional, through the restructuring of the form of local government, including the creation of new unitary authorities or merging council administrations, as well as involving a range of direct activities to meet specific needs such as for housing and to generate more income through property acquisition and investment to provide a more secure and balanced income stream for the future. The extent to which local authorities have engaged in these asset and income generation approaches has varied, as we have found. However, it is also the case that, while starting with some initiatives, councils have continued to extend their activities in a cumulative way, as they gain more confidence and learn from others.

While the period of austerity for local authorities that started in 2010 was accompanied by uncertainty and responses to service and staff cutting that had been used before, the scale of the government's programme for reducing funding for local authorities was on a scale that had not been seen before (NAO, 2019). The government sought to use the financial weakness of local government, which subsequently followed, to impose a more centralised approach to the selection and delivery of its preferred projects through a programme of 'deals' – city deals and growth deals for example – but these were not enough to fill the gaps and required resources to develop and implement them that local authorities no longer had. Meanwhile, the basic services were increasingly closed, passed to the management of the community or reduced to the bare minimum.

Latterly in this period, the government diverted its attention to Brexit, and since 2016, the internal Conservative Party dynamics and its parliamentary challenges have left local authorities to fend for themselves. The local authority Revenue Support Grant (RSG) continued to reduce on its waning taper with the prospect of final closure of the RSG in 2020. At the same time, in the Homelessness Reduction Act 2017, all councils were given greater responsibilities for those who might become homeless. The increasing costs of responding to unregulated landlord behaviour placed further strain on council finances, continuing the trend of what Peter John refers to as a century and a half of central government giving local authorities 'tasks that it does not want to carry out itself because they are troublesome or politically contentious or both, which allows it to shift blame if it needs to' (John, 2014: 697). Further, the planning reforms that were introduced in 2012 through the NPPF (DCLG, 2012) placed even greater reliance on the development of market housing to provide affordable housing. The methodologies for defining the needs for, in effect, market housing in each local authority area through the

NPPF became more separated and increasingly different from local authority assessments of housing need. These demonstrate housing needs to support health and wider local economic objectives. For many local authorities this all presented a bleak future for their councils, finances, communities and people.

As our research has demonstrated, the response of local authorities to this situation has, in many cases, been proactive, innovative and surprising. This book has discussed the more detailed motivations for this range of activities and their manifestations through a range of local initiatives. However, in this last chapter we wish to discuss four issues that arise as a result of these local authority initiatives. The first is one that we are often asked: how far will local authority direct housing provision really be able to contribute to the supply of housing across England? Can the local authority ever return to its position as a key provider of new housing as it was before 1980? The second question is whether this local authority focus on creating a secure financial platform for the future will change the nature of central–local relations in England. If councils do not have to rely on central government for funding to run services, can this make them less at risk of being buffeted by changes in government policy, and dependent on 'deals' and competitions, and more able to address their own priorities for their communities? Third, what are the areas of risk potentially associated with this seeming system-level shift in local authority funding and approaches to local authority finance, including in relation to issues of social justice and geographical variation? And finally, we reflect on wider questions of how this might be conceptualised for future academic consideration.

How far can local authority housing delivery extend?

As we have shown extensively in this book, a particular feature of the response of local authorities to super-austerity and the housing crisis has been a resurgence in local authority direct delivery of housing. A common question is how far this activity extends in terms of the number of dwellings and how far it might extend in future; this is unsurprising given the overwhelming focus on housing supply in the UK. Statistics from the Ministry of Housing, Communities and Local Government (MHCLG) provide some useful indications in terms of the activity directly by local authorities under their HRA or general fund activity. Table 213 of MHCLG (2020) shows the number of new-build dwellings completed by local authorities through their HRA. In 2018–19 there were 2,450 such new homes, growing steadily from 1,490 in 2015–16, 1,530 in 2016–17 and 1,730 in 2017–18, the highest number since 1990–91. The number of new-build dwellings started by local authorities in 2018–19 was 2,540, also having grown steadily from 1,900 in 2015–16, 1,830 in 2016–17 and 2,000 in 2017–18, and the highest number since 1992–93, although still low compared to the 128,880 new-build dwellings completed by local authorities and the 135,700 started in 1969–70. These figures do not include housing completed by local authorities using other methods such as companies or joint ventures. Table 253 of MHCLG (2020) breaks this down by local authority and shows that the most new dwellings completed by a local authority in 2018–19 were the 390 in Hackney, with more than 100 each completed by Cornwall, Darlington, Ealing, Hillingdon, Sandwell, Telford and Wrekin, Walsall and Wiltshire. Overall, 66 local authorities had completed or started building new dwellings in 2018–19 funded through the HRA. This includes authorities of all types (districts, unitary authorities, boroughs), and urban and rural authorities located in all parts of England.

Another indicator of local authority activity is the MHCLG live table 1000 (MHCLG, 2020), which charts additional affordable housing supply that includes social rent built using the HRA together with other affordable housing provided through shared ownership and other planning contributions. Table 5.1 summarises the figures in relation to supply within each local authority. This shows an uplift in supply, from 3,468

Table 5.1: New supply of affordable housing attributed to local authority direct provision across England over the past four years

Type of affordable housing	2015–16	2016–17	2017–18	2018–19
Social rent	1,521	1,473	1,225	1,445
London affordable rent	0	0	54	137
Affordable rent	1,608	2,465	3,149	3,308
Intermediate rent	149	25	24	16
Shared ownership	95	98	220	309
Affordable homeownership	95	35	0	26
Total	**3,468**	**4,096**	**4,672**	**5,241**

Source: MHCLG (2020, live table 1000)

new affordable homes in 2015–16 to 5,241 in 2018–19. These figures only account for local authority completions under their HRA and through planning agreements. There are no centrally collated figures from government on the activity of local authority housing companies, which may be included in the 'private enterprise' figures on new supply and some authorities are reluctant to disclose the number of units their companies have built, potentially for commercial operating reasons. However, if we look at those authorities that did disclose the number of units they had built through all means, including under the HRA, general fund and through a joint venture or wholly-owned company, and then assume these are representative of all authorities that said in our survey they were directly delivering housing, then an estimation can be made. Eighty-three authorities responded to that part of our survey, from which we identified a combined total of 8,992 homes delivered by local authorities and their companies: 3,803 affordable (42%), 2,079 social (23%), 943 intermediate (10%), 1,428 for sale (16%) and 739 private rented sector (8%). For those that did respond, the mean average homes delivered was 99. The median average units delivered was 55. Assuming 69% of all authorities in England were delivering housing, and those delivering had each delivered 55 units last year, this would suggest that more than 13,000 new homes were delivered last year inclusive of activity by local authority companies.

There is clearly, then, rapidly developing activity. From a small start, we are seeing an encouraging increase in the number of new homes and the number of affordable homes supplied by local authorities, including directly through their HRA (if they have one) and through their housing companies (if they have one). From our roundtable discussions, we also know it can easily take three years from identifying a site as suitable for housing to getting onsite to build, so would envisage further growth in future as more local authorities are entering this area of activity.

It is important, however, to note the significant challenges and barriers that exist around authorities engaging in directly delivering housing again. Not having retained stock, as already mentioned, is a significant – but not impossible – barrier. Those that retained stock have useful skills in-house in relation to housing delivery and management. In response to a question on our survey about delivering more housing, the most common response related to a lack of land. For various reasons, local authority land holdings vary considerably. Taking a proactive approach may identify more sites than have first been realised as suitable for housing as demonstrated by Plymouth, Bristol and Preston Councils. Small sites can bring their own financial and delivery challenges unless developed as a package or placed on the local self-build register. Volume housebuilders tend to avoid small sites. Nevertheless, the finances of delivering housing – particularly affordable housing – are easiest when the local authority owns the land and those local authorities with more land are at an advantage.

There are other key concerns. If financing housing development by borrowing, the effects of loan repayments on revenue for day-to-day service delivery within the authority (particularly given the government's increase in PWLB interest rates in 2019) and also skills can be an issue. There are specific skills relating to housing development and delivery which authorities have not necessarily emphasised over recent decades when building few houses. Local authorities will be competing against private developers and housing associations for those skills. In London, the Mayor's Homebuilding Capacity Fund is helping local authorities acquire staff with the right skills again (Mayor of London, 2018) but local authorities in the rest of England are receiving much less support for this. However, we did find, through our roundtables and case studies, an increasing number of local authorities with access to development surveyors with commercial experience. This is through direct appointment – full or part-time, through shared appointments with other councils, consultancy contracts or joint ventures. These development surveyors can make an important contribution to housing delivery and maximising affordable housing supply through both direct delivery and viability assessment negotiations in planning.

Local authorities without an HRA (and those with) may consider building through a local authority housing company as an option, but again in our research, local authorities acknowledges challenges around understanding company as opposed to local authorities roles, the time required to establish a company and, again, specific development skills. If trying to subsidise affordable housing through market housing, local authorities may well be able to deliver a higher percentage than private developers if they are willing to reduce their profit or surplus margin or are able to start with their own land. However, there can still be viability issues. Even if provided by local authorities, the national need for affordable housing is unlikely to be met as a residual from the gains associated with developing market housing through the planning system.

Local authorities are scaling up their own provision of housing, and there are numerous examples of good practice and successful delivery across the country, with models and approaches reflecting local circumstances and innovation. There are reasons to be optimistic, but also challenges. We believe that the current rates of delivery are likely to continue to increase over the coming years. However, in relation to affordable housing in particular, we understand many authorities are continuing to lose more units to RTB than they are able to build (although national-level statistics on this are harder to access). In Nottingham, for example, Nottingham City Homes, the council's housing arm, is losing one home to RTB for every day of the year. With homes sold at enforced discounts and restrictions on the use of the receipts, local authorities still face a difficult battle to retain enough social rented affordable housing. Unless RTB is abolished, and unless there is larger grant funding available to support the delivery of affordable housing, then national need as experienced at the local level is unlikely to be met.

A new form of central–local relations?

Since 1979, the role of local government as a core component of the welfare state apparatus for supporting communities and people has been increasingly undermined. The removal of housing development following the International Monetary Fund crisis (1976) and of housing stock after 1979, started to undermine the core function and role of local authorities for many communities. This had been a central activity and community safety net since 1919. It was part of the post-war fulfilment of the military covenant. It was also an example of local authorities wanting to deliver the government's agenda in a compliant way. The Thatcher policy to introduce RTB switched this local authority role from being reassuring and supportive in providing housing to one that was defined by the state as getting in the way, hoarding assets that belonged to the people and keeping them from fulfilling their personal objectives of homeownership. Not only was the rhetoric devised to create this division but the system for future development, repayment of costs from RTB receipts and meeting social needs in the local community through housing was removed. From this point onwards, local and central government were no longer partners in the delivery of the welfare state but in opposition to each other (Kettle, 2020). The implementation of CCT, the increasing removal of mainstream funding to be replaced by competitive pre-determined expenditure schemes, increasingly made local authorities dependent on central government for both their agendas and the funding to deliver them. The introduction of Osborne's austerity was the final act in this long wave of policy, with central government's detachment from local government nearing some kind of final form. Local government shifted from being a partner to a sector, no different from any other. It was perhaps both this and the government's distraction with Brexit that created the conditions for local authorities to find their own ways to try to create their financial security so that this kind of dependency could not be recreated in the future.

The examination of the role of local authorities delivering housing that is at the heart of this book has focused on the contractual relationship between central and local government to achieve this that has existed since the creation of modern local government in the 1880s. As local government is not part of the British constitution as in other countries of the Organisation for Economic Co-operation and Development (OECD), then its funding, powers and legitimacy have been dependent on the prevailing political ideology of the government in power. The provision of public housing funded by the government but delivered by local authorities was one of the fullest expressions of this contractual relationship. It was based on a societal and later welfarist consensus of the function of the state and the role of local authorities in its delivery. The emergence of Thatcherism demonstrated how fragile this seemingly normative relationship was, and how quickly it could be weakened and, in the case of housing provision, largely dismantled. The government was no longer willing to use local authorities in basic welfare state provision.

The removal of powers, funding and assets from local authorities put them in a dependent relationship with government, which can be likened to colonial or parent–child models. Some of this has been politically driven, but it has also involved central government civil servants: former Minister Nick Raynsford has argued that central government civil servants view local government with distrust and treat it with contempt (Foster, 2016). The role of the UK's membership of the European Union (EU), in introducing the principle of subsidiarity through the Treaties of Rome (1957), Maastricht (1992) and Lisbon (2009), started to embed devolved practices in the UK state including for local authorities. For local government, this is most clearly evidenced in their most recent manifestation, combined authorities with directly elected mayors (Morphet, 2018). However, these subsidiarity principles were not included as structural reforms in the British constitution. Unlike other countries, in the UK, devolved parliaments, assemblies and local authorities continue to exist at the behest of Parliament and have their powers determined by the state. The introduction of austerity in 2010, at the same time that the principle of subsidiarity was required to be applied to local authorities in the 2009 Lisbon Treaty, was a simultaneous attempt to increase the dependency of local authorities on the state rather than to enable them to be autonomous. Local authorities could have more power over less money.

Government accepted that the application of this EU subsidiarity principle meant that it could no longer prescribe what local authorities could do. However, in reducing local authority funding (NAO, 2019) and introducing a 'deal' culture, meant that the government's centrally predetermined priorities could be guaranteed through local authorities 'voluntarily' bidding to deliver them. Sections 1 to 7 of the Localism Act 2011 gave some further powers to local authorities to behave in the same way as private sector organisations. This was accompanied by changes in accounting procedures through the application of the International Financial Reporting Standard (IFRS) to bring the private and public sectors into line on both revenue and capital accounting. The government's international commitment to apply the IFRS in the UK might have brought an end to the HRA and replaced it with the same capital accounting rules that apply to local authorities in other countries of the OECD and in business. However, the government has declined to implement this element of the international agreement it made on IFRS, leaving the HRA intact as a politically structured concept for managing social housing by local authorities, even if it removed the borrowing cap in 2018. In addition to all of this, the UK's departure from the EU means the end of the treaty obligations on the UK to apply subsidiarity and the government will be free to return to direct control measures on local authority powers, funding and programmes without having to use 'deals' to justify its centralised approach.

Faced with this level of austerity and a competitive culture for deal funding, which sometimes takes years to determine individual bid outcomes, local authorities unsurprisingly want to find ways to secure and guarantee their income each year without the continual shocks of government policy and indeterminate delivery programmes. The result is a re-emergence of municipal entrepreneurialism, across a range of activities (as shown in Chapter Four). While this remains in its relative infancy, local authorities are undertaking different forms of this entrepreneurialism, based on their local priorities, culture and existing asset bases. The culture of each local authority is an important determinant of the type of municipal entrepreneurialism that they are likely to pursue. Some councils want to be leaders in general while others take leadership in specific policy areas and these change over time. The councils that are ambitious for change and delivery will be led by councillors and officers who share a commitment, and this overcomes internal or silo-driven objectives that may be pursued by other departments. The continuation of leading-edge initiatives will depend on their success in practice and political leaders may fall if their policies are not shown to deliver as intended. These leading councils demonstrate that higher risks may be taken if the rewards follow. Political leaders are supported by officers who find ways to implement their objectives, attracted to work for councils that are active in specific policy delivery. These officers may also be innovative in their approaches, examining legislation, different financing schemes and methods of delivery outside more traditional approaches.

Most councils, however, take a more cautious view and do not want to be at the leading edge. There are costs and risks associated with being the 'first'. This may be because their political make-up is more susceptible to change at local elections or because they have little experience in the kind of approaches that are being used by the leaders of the policy field in other local authorities. In these cases, council leaders will review the approaches of others, learn from their mistakes and consider the 'best fit' between the range of initiatives on offer, their specific local needs and what might be politically and organisationally achievable in their areas. They will also have an eye on the views of the community. At the same time, the bulk of council politicians, particularly leaders, are not immune from the influence of competition between councils for attention and praise. Few councils want a reputation for doing little for their communities and most politicians need to demonstrate what has been achieved at each election cycle. In some smaller councils, these cycles run in three of every four years. This makes it more difficult to find longer delivery slots, in comparison with councils elected for four years, but at the same time maintains the pressure to demonstrate that politicians are addressing local concerns on the doorstep when canvassing for local electoral support. Our research shows that local electorates have the view that councils should be providing housing of all types of need and cannot understand why this is not being delivered. This political support across all political parties and geographies has been a stimulus to municipal entrepreneurialism in the majority of councils. The role of local authorities in providing housing has now returned as a mainstream objective but there is little or no expectation that this will be provided by any more than minimal levels of government grant. In exploring the varieties of municipal entrepreneurialism to provide housing, councils are also seeking a more secure financial, economic and social future for their areas. Will this longer-term financial independence of local authorities change the balance of the central–local relationship?

As with all processes of change, there is also a range of countervailing pressures that influence how change is viewed and implemented. Since 2010, government has taken a largely benign approach to local authorities providing housing again, not least as it has recognised that the shortfall in meeting its own published housing delivery objectives cannot be reached by the private sector alone (NAO, 2019). However, while direct provision of housing together with the acquisition of asset portfolios have been significant in creating longer-term financial security, the government has also revisited more strategic approaches to reforming local authorities. In 2007, the Sub National Review of Economic Development and Regeneration (HM Treasury, 2007) proposed larger, more strategic local authorities led by stronger political leaders and, in time, directly elected mayors. The creation of local enterprise partnerships in 2010 helped government to nudge local authorities into the practices of working at this more strategic scale without having any formal process of local government review. In 2012, all local authorities in England were invited to bid for 'devolution deal' funding that would be administered by groups of councils if they worked together at this strategic scale. Although there was little initial progress in the implementation of these devolution deals, apart from the creation of ten new combined authorities, these have now been dusted off following the 2019 general election.

As part of implementing its devolution policies for 'levelling up' the country, the government is proposing a range of specific deals across England. These include the creation of new larger unitary local authorities within new combined authorities with directly elected mayors, with deals being offered across England including Cumbria, Lancashire, West Yorkshire and North Yorkshire, with others expected to follow. These larger authorities will have access to greater funding and the ability to employ more experienced professional staff. There may be short-term pauses on the policies to implement housing using the entrepreneurialism models discussed here. If the government is not confined in its relationships with local authorities by the application of EU subsidiarity principles, then these new larger local authorities may have more focus on delivering government priorities and less on meeting local needs. Yet the divergence of the institutional requirements on the planning system to provide land for market housing and the increased needs for all types of housing that are not being met by the market suggest that local authorities may not give up their new-found energy for housing provision quite so easily. Further, the establishment of larger local authorities with greater financial independence indicates a greater challenge to the government of the day (Richards, 2018). Government will also need mechanisms and delivery vehicles to meet the Paris Climate Accord targets, which can only be met by the retrofitting of the existing stock of buildings in any area, particularly of housing. Which organisations will deliver this if not local authorities?

Finally, the government's centralised response to COVID-19 has ignored local authorities and local public health systems including general practitioners. As a local approach is recommended by the World Health Organization (WHO) and has been the basis of those countries with far lower death and infection rates, the UK government's approach for England has been increasingly seen as one that has privatised the pandemic for supporter gains (Monbiot, 2020). Yet, in the end, it will be local authorities not privatised service companies that will have to resolve the localised outbreaks of the virus, as in every other country. This demonstrates the continuing poor relationship between central and local government in England, and the desperate need for more financial security and independence for local authorities in future (as is in place in countries like Germany that have more successfully managed the pandemic).

Risks and challenges

Discussion of central government's view of local government highlights that there are risks and challenges facing local authorities on their journey to new models of funding. A key risk is that of central government interference. The activity around municipal enterprises, particularly housing companies, has grown organically from local authority innovation and sharing of ideas and best practice between themselves rather than having been imposed top-down. As already noted, it has happened at a time that central government in the UK has been distracted. However, there are signs that the government may revert to centralisation and try to re-exert control over local government. As we write this conclusion, the UK 2020 budget has just been published and has announced a review of the PWLB due to 'a minority of councils' using the 'cheap finance to buy very significant amounts of commercial property for rental income' (HM Treasury, 2020). The same budget, incidentally, repeated the untruth that the planning system, constraining land availability, is the most significant barrier to building more housing. Central government maintains strict control over rates of council tax that authorities can raise, and resists consideration of more progressive measures like increasing top-rate council tax for the most valuable properties (on a current, rather than 1993, valuation) or allowing the introduction of a local government income tax.

Local authorities are, then, in a difficult position, of central government restricting their ability to raise money through taxation, but also apparently taking a dim view of some of the attempts to raise funds through more commercial activities.

Entering the realm of more commercial activity also has its own risks and challenges, of course, beyond central government's controlling tendencies. There are levels of financial risk associated with commercial enterprise. The risks may be higher around commercial property investment than housing, particularly in a post-COVID world. Looking back into Birmingham's history, Skelcher (2017) argues that the benefits of the municipalisation of the gas company were contested, and that following the economic downturn of the 1880s, the city council was left with significant debts and unutilised land around its New Street redevelopment scheme as investors were less willing to become engaged. More recently, looking across all types of council companies, Ferry et al (2018) found evidence of 20 companies having been closed in 2016/ 17. Our own desk survey also found evidence of 16 housing/ property companies that appeared to have closed from 2017 to 2019. Derbyshire County Council's housing development company appears to have ceased operations, demonstrating the challenges around financing and skills that can occur, particularly when a council has no HRA from which to build. Some volume housebuilders make extremely high levels of profit, but often they have built up internal skills capacity over many years, are willing to aggressively ignore local plan policies, try to minimise affordable housing contributions, ignore small sites and build at lower quality in a way that a local authority-owned company may be unable or (hopefully) unwilling to do.

As well as the levels of financial risk that can go with any commercial endeavour, there are also more practical considerations associated with establishing council companies. Looking at experience in Continental Europe, Vroon et al (2017) argue that there is a need for clarity about relationships between the company and the local authority, and well-defined goals for the company, but often these are not present and there can be political conflicts around these. This leads to a high initial failure rate for municipally owned corporations. The conflict over goals can certainly be seen in relation to some local housing companies, for example the difficulties of trying to balance the demand to build at higher quality and maximise affordable housing contributions while also making a profit to generate income for the council.

The nature of the relationship between the company and the council also raises the issue of the democratic accountability of some companies and their activities, and potential conflicts of interest, as raised by Beswick and Penny (2018), Christophers (2019) and Ferry et al (2018). Ferry et al are particularly concerned about when companies are being used to provide what had been local authority services, commenting that '[t]he extent to which local authority services are now the responsibility of these wholly- or partly-owned companies has implications for the community and especially capacity of citizens to exercise their civic and democratic rights, for example in challenging issues of poor performance or governance' (Ferry et al, 2018: 478). The debate is, perhaps, slightly different where companies are being used not to provide services but to raise revenue for services, for example through new areas of activity, but the concern is a fair one and the financial, democratic and political risks of new commercial interventionism will clearly require careful management.

One way to consider this is in relation to principles of good governance, such as those published by the Council of Europe (2018). In relation to those, it is important to note that there are actually potential benefits from some of the activity considered in this book, for example related to efficiency and effectiveness (making best possible use of resources, for example, it is surely better to build housing on council land than just sell it to a private developer to do that), competence and capacity (new activity to transform skills into capacity to produce better results), innovation and openness to change (examples of new and efficient solutions to problems), sustainability and long-term orientation (a more secure financial income stream provides an ability to secure a long-term future of service to the local community) and sound financial management (arguably there are some benefits around undertaking activity to increase income streams not dependent on central government for resources and revenues). However, there are potential issues related to the principles of openness and transparency (particularly if commercial sensitivities common to a company mean there is less publicly available information, as you might expect with a local authority), ethical conduct (in relation to the potential for conflicts of interest) and sound financial management (in relation to commercial risks and the potential undermining of inter-municipal solidarity).

There does appear to be an erosion of the 'principle of equalisation', which has been a longstanding feature of UK local government finance (Hastings et al, 2017). There is a geography to this new urban entrepreneurialism, which, while lacking, the nation-state universalism of the old managerialism still remains located within the drivers and constraints of national frameworks and where the resilience to austerity can depend very much on intensely localised advantages, historic assets and variable resources, such as land holdings and the presence or absence of retained council housing stock (Lowndes and Gardner, 2016; Phelps and Miao, 2019). It is understandable that questions of social and, indeed, spatial justice are raised by a move from central government grant funding to more local authority entrepreneurial activity as a source of finance. The geographies of this are, however, complex. London boroughs have faced some of the largest decreases in funding through the abolition of the RSG but have been some of the most proactive local authorities in building housing again; some authorities in more generally deprived areas have successfully invested outwith their boundaries in investment properties. The issues with social and spatial justice are most likely to arise, however, if some authorities are not able to establish successful revenue-raising enterprises, or in the event of a commercial enterprise failing.

Understanding the new municipal entrepreneurialism

As we discussed in Chapter One, a variety of labels and concepts can be brought to bear to understand the response of local government in England to the twin crises of super-austerity and housing. It is useful to situate these processes within a wider understanding of political economy. As Skelcher (2017: 937) has argued in relation to Birmingham, the cuts from 2010 onwards provide 'the material economic context for the City Council's switch to a path of corporatisation', with the political economy within which a local authority is located creating the conditions within which its leadership makes choices on how they can possible respond. Clearly, the crisis of super-austerity for local authorities has been brought about by a political choice by a central government that has often been sceptical about the role of the state and so, as Penny (2017: 1358) has commented, 'local government is once again being used to absorb and resolve the crisis tendencies of neoliberal capitalist accumulation and uneven development through local governance innovation'. The notion of neoliberalism, even in a zombified form, helps us understand the situation local government now finds itself in (Peck, 2010, in Green and Lavery, 2018).

Similarly, the concept of 'financialisation' helps us understand more broadly how housing has become seen as more of an investment vehicle, valued for its exchange rather than use value, and the demand-side drivers of the housing crisis, as well as an increasing reliance by public authorities on investment vehicles and financial capital flows even where these are beneficial to local public services (albeit there has been a much longer history to many of these processes, as illustrated by looking at housing development and the local state in the 19th century). However, these broad concepts can only get us so far in considering the differentiated 'actually existing' responses of local authorities across England, many of which show considerable variation that can be overlooked by such a grouping together under one label. Indeed, local authorities selling land to private developers have been critiqued under the banner of financialisation, but so has the direct development of their own land where the income generated is for a social purpose. Both interpretations are not necessarily incorrect but raise the issue of how far the concept takes us in understanding what is going on in practice. Thompson et al write that:

> Financialising housing and other fixed public infrastructures as liquid assets to generate alternative sources of revenue for austerity-choked councils is a highly creative coping mechanism … [but] this represents a problematic and contradictory commodification of public goods in order to fund other public goods. Municipal entrepreneurialism stokes the fire of financialisation. (Thompson et al, 2020: 21; see also Thompson, 2020)

The activity of some of the early local housing companies (such as the example given by Beswick and Penny, 2018) does seem to have been in the category of urban speculation (after Phelps and Miao, 2019). Some joint ventures sought to redevelop council housing estates in schemes that reduced the amount of social and affordable housing in preference over income generation, for both the council and the developers. This potentially led to the regressive displacement of communities and local government complicity in speculative real estate development, although each case varies. In some locations, local authority tenants were moved a short distance to improved or new homes. Interestingly, in July 2018, Haringey Council decided to abandon its planned £4 billion 50:50 joint venture with LendLease (as a company through the Haringey Development Vehicle Plan) to redevelop council-owned land and property in the borough (Hill, 2018; Williams, 2018; Hollander, 2019). This also reflects a wider shift in Labour Party policy about such so-called 'estate regeneration', frequently involving local authority companies and their own social housing estates being turned over for more market housing (Chakrabortty, 2017) in order to generate more income and guaranteed housing supply in their areas. These plans were formulated at the height of recession when there were fast diminishing funds for local authorities and a government antipathetic to local government. Most local authorities that embarked down this road, for estate and site redevelopment with joint venture partners, have stated that they would take a different approach now.

Other commentators also take a more sympathetic view in recognising these local authority austerity dilemmas. Contrasting the tendency to have a 'bright side' of public service innovation in public administration literature, with the 'dark side' tendencies of the literature on urban entrepreneurialism, neoliberalisation and financialisation, Phelps and Miao (2019) suggest that the key factor is whether there is discernible evidence of gains being put to uses beneficial to the public good. Some of the inventive and innovatory activity of the local state can have progressive potential. Phelps and Miao (2019) categorise local authority housing companies as 'urban intrapreneurialism', that is, defined by processes of innovation and invention within a public organisation, and suggest that, on balance, the effects are likely to be progressive. There is some similarity here to Christophers (2019), who focuses his critique on central rather than local government. For shaping the financial context within which English local authorities must now respond, he believes many risks have been over-played and that there is often an underlying and unfair assumption that the public sector is commercially incompetent. He highlights, using Morphet and Clifford (2017) as evidence, that local authorities are making difficult choices in very challenging financial circumstances in order to protect services and strive for positive socioeconomic ends.

The over-reliance of UK local government on central government funding has often suggested the lack of autonomy that follows from this. However, as we have found, the very nature of local government allows for the possibility of local variation and a basis on which alternatives become possible (see also Ward et al, 2015). Some local authorities are responding positively to the challenging circumstances they find themselves in. Others are not as yet but may yet adopt more progressive practices to help them serve their communities. The scale of local authority housing activity found by our research suggests that more proactive local authorities are in the making. The majority of local authorities have taken a different approach from that suggested by some critics. They have not reduced affordable housing but are attempting to build more and to use market housing to generate income for a social purpose. Understanding the variation in approaches is important before applying sweeping criticism.

Municipal entrepreneurialism does not provide all the answers for local authorities and there can be no return to a mythical golden age. However, austerity has encouraged a deeper consideration of the range of powers and methods open to councils for investment, delivery to meet needs and longer-term financial security. The role of housing in opening up this potential for operating differently has been paramount. If it was the introduction of the RTB scheme into local authority housing in 1979 that commenced the era of local authority decline in England, the opportunities provided by municipal entrepreneurialism, led by housing again, could introduce the next phase of municipal independence.

References

Aalbers, M. 2015. The great moderation, the great excess and the global housing crisis, *International Journal of Housing Policy*, 15(1), pp 43–60.

Aalbers, M. 2017. The variegated financialization of housing. *International Journal of Urban and Regional Research*, 41(4), pp 542–554.

Adnett, N. and Hardy, S. 1998. The impact of TUPE on compulsory competitive tendering: evidence from employers, *Local Government Studies*, 24(3), pp 36–50.

Ahrens, T. and Ferry, L. 2018. Institutional entrepreneurship, practice memory, and cultural memory choice and creativity in the pursuit of endogenous change of local authority budgeting, *Management Accounting Research*, 38, pp 12–21.

Aldridge, M. 2017. *The British New Towns: A programme without a policy*. Abingdon: Routledge.

Allen, C. 2008. *Housing market renewal and social class*. London: Routledge.

Allen, G.R. 1951. The growth of industry on trading estates, 1920–39, with special reference to Slough Trading Estate, *Oxford Economic Papers*, 3(3), pp 272–300.

Armstrong, H. 2015. Local energy in an age of austerity. *Preserving the value of local and community energy*. London: Nesta.

Ascher K. 1987. *The politics of privatisation: Contracting out public services*. London: Macmillan.

Bailey, N. and Robertson, D. 1997. Housing renewal, urban policy and gentrification, *Urban Studies*, 34(4), pp 561–578.

Bailey, N., Bramley, G. and Hastings, A. 2015. Symposium introduction: local responses to 'austerity', *Local Government Studies*, 41(4), 571–581.

Balchin, P. 1998. An overview of pre-Thatcherite housing policy, in Balchin, P., and Rhoden, M. eds., *Housing: The essential foundations* (pp 1–24). London: Taylor & Francis.

Ball, M. 1983. *Housing policy and economic power: The political economy of owner occupation*. London: Routledge.

Ball, M. 2011. Planning delay and the responsiveness of English housing supply, *Urban Studies*, 48(2), pp 349–362.

Barker, K. 2004. *Barker review of housing supply*. HM Treasury. www. barkerreview.org.uk

Barker, K. 2006. *Barker review of land use planning: Final report, recommendations*. London: The Stationery Office.

Barker, N. 2018. The HRA borrowing cap explained. www. insidehousing.co.uk/insight/insight/the-hra-borrowing-cap-explained-58486 [Accessed 11.03.2020].

Barker, N. 2019. Birmingham Council's housing company to build 2,708 homes by 2029. www.insidehousing.co.uk/news/news/birmingham-councils-housing-company-to-build-2708-homes-by-2029-61463 [Accessed 11.03.2020].

Barlow, M. 1940. *Report of the Royal Commission on the Distribution of the Industrial Population*. London: The Stationery Office.

Beswick, J., Alexandri, G., Byrne, M., Vives-Miró, S., Fields, D., Hodkinson, S., and Janoschka, M. 2016. Speculating on London's housing future: The rise of global corporate landlords in 'post-crisis' urban landscapes. *City*, 20(2), pp 321–341.

Beswick, J. and Penny, J. 2018. Demolishing the present to sell off the future? The emergence of 'financialized municipal entrepreneurialism' in London, *International Journal of Urban and Regional Research*, 42(4), pp 612–632.

Bingham, M. 2001. Policy utilisation in planning control: planning appeals in England's 'plan-led' system, *Town Planning Review*, 72(3), pp 321–340.

Birmingham City Council. 2020. Birmingham Business Charter for Social Responsibility. www.birmingham.gov.uk/info/50209/birmingham_business_charter_for_social_responsibility [Accessed 11.03.2020].

Blakeley, G. 2019. The UK's local authorities are at breaking point. But municipal socialism could save them, *New Statesman*, 3 May.

Booth, P. and Huxley, M. 2012. 1909 and all that: reflections on the Housing, Town Planning, Etc. Act 1909, *Planning Perspectives*, 27(2), pp 267–283.

Borges, W., Clarke, H.D., Stewart, M.C., Sanders, D. and Whiteley, P. 2013. The emerging political economy of austerity in Britain, *Electoral Studies*, 32(3), pp 396–403.

Boughton, J. 2018. *Municipal dreams: The rise and fall of council housing*. London: Verso Books.

Brady, D. 2018. PWLB rule change leaves councils 'struggling to pay loans'. www.publicfinance.co.uk/news/2018/05/pwlb-rule-change-leaves-councils-struggling-pay-loans [Accessed 29.07.2020].

Bresnen, M.J., Wray, K., Bryman, A., Beardsworth, A.D., Ford, J.R. and Keil, E.T. 1985. The flexibility of recruitment in the construction industry: formalisation or re-casualisation? *Sociology*, 19(1), pp 108–124.

Buckingham and Windsor Advertiser. 2018. Aylesbury Vale District Council closes Limecart and Incgen company. www.buckinghamtoday.co.uk/business/aylesbury-vale-district-council-closes-limecart-and-incgen-company-713871 [Accessed 12.03.2020].

Bullock, N. 2002. *Building the post-war world: Modern architecture and reconstruction in Britain*. Hove: Psychology Press.

Bunar, N. 2010. The controlled school market and urban schools in Sweden, *Journal of School Choice*, 4(1), pp 47–73.

Burgess, G. and Monk, S. 2016. Delivering planning obligations—are agreements successfully delivered?, in *Planning gain: Providing infrastructure and affordable housing* (pp 201–226), Crook, T., Henneberry J., and Whitehead. Oxford: C. Wiley Blackwell.

Burgess, G., Monk, S., Whitehead, C.M.E. and Crook, A.D.H. 2007. *How local planning authorities are delivering policies for affordable housing*. York: Joseph Rowntree Foundation.

Burns, W. 1963. *New towns for old: The technique of urban renewal*. New York: L. Hill.

Butcher, H., Law, I.G., Leach, R. and Mullard, M. 1990. *Local government and Thatcherism*. London: Routledge.

Cain, J. 2018. Teesside councils allowing more homes to be built than they need to – are there too many? www.gazettelive.co.uk/news/property/teesside-councils-building-more-homes-15037844 [Accessed 17.12.2019].

Carr-West, J. 2017. Why did the tri-borough fail? Public Finance. 12 May. www.publicfinance.co.uk/opinion/2017/05/why-did-triborough-fail [Accessed 22.11.2019].

Casselden, B., Pickard, A., Walton, G. and McLeod, J. 2017. Keeping the doors open in an age of austerity? Qualitative analysis of stakeholder views on volunteers in public libraries, *Journal of Librarianship and Information Science*, 47(3), pp 187–203.

Chakrabortty, A. 2017. Jeremy Corbyn has declared war on Labour councils over housing. www.theguardian.com/commentisfree/2017/sep/27/jeremy-corbyn-labour-councils-housing [Accessed 13.03.2020].

Chakrabortty, A. 2018. In 2011 Preston hit rock bottom. Then it took back control, *The Guardian*, 31 January. www.theguardian.com/commentisfree/2018/jan/31/preston-hit-rock-bottom-took-back-control

Chandler, J.A. 2010. A rationale for local government. *Local Government Studies*, *36*(1), 5-20.

Chandler, J.A. 2013. *Explaining local government: Local government in Britain since 1800*. Manchester: Manchester University Press.

Christophers, B. 2015. The limits to financialization, *Dialogues in Human Geography*, 5(2), pp 183–200.

Christophers, B. 2018. *The new enclosure*. London: Verso.

Christophers, B. 2019. Putting financialisation in its financial context: transformations in local government-led urban development in post-financial crisis England, *Transactions of the Institute of British Geographers*, 44(3), pp 571–586.

CIPFA (Chartered Institute of Public Finance and Accountancy). 2019. Prudential Property Investment draft CIPFA guidance on the application of the prudential framework June 2019,

Civica/CIPFA. 2016. The commercial imperative. www.cipfa.org/policy-and-guidance/reports/civica-the-commercial-imperative [Accessed 29.07.2020].

Clapson, M. 1998. *Invincible green suburbs, brave new towns: Social change and urban dispersal in postwar England*. Manchester: Manchester University Press.

Clarke, M. and Stewart, J. 2003. Handling the wicked issues, *The Managing Care Reader*, 273, p 280.

Clayton, J. and Donavan, C. 2016. Distancing and limited resourcefulness: third sector service provision under austerity: localism in the north east of England, *Urban Studies*, 53(4), pp 723–740.

Clegg, L. and Farstad, F. 2019. The local political economy of the regulatory state: governing affordable housing in England, *Regulation & Governance*.

Clifford, B. 2018. Freedom of information request to support Work Package 2: charting outsourcing in UK public planning. http://witpi.group.shef.ac.uk/wp-content/uploads/2019/02/WITPI-FoI-Research-Overview-2.pdf [Accessed 11.03.2020].

Clifford, B., Ferm, J., Livingstone, N. and Canelas, P. 2019. *Understanding the impacts of deregulation in planning*. Basingstoke: Palgrave Pivot.

Cochrane, A. 1991. The changing state of local government: restructuring for the 1990s, *Public Administration*, 69(3), pp 281–302.

Collison, P. 1963. *The Cutteslowe Walls: A study in social class*. London: Faber and Faber.

Companies House. 2020. Search the register. https://beta.companieshouse.gov.uk/ [Accessed 11.03.2020].

Copley, T. 2019. *Right to Buy: Wrong for London*. London: Greater London Assembly.

Coq-Huelva, D. 2013. Urbanisation and financialisation in the context of a rescaling state: The case of Spain. *Antipode*, 45(5), 1213–1231.

Corkindale, J. 2007. Planning gain or missed opportunity? The Barker review of land use planning, *Economic Affairs*, 27(3), pp 46–51.

Council of Europe 2018. 12 principles of good governance. www.coe.int/en/web/good-governance/12-principles [Accessed 29.07.2020]

Cowan, D. 2019. Reducing homelessness or re-ordering the deckchairs? *The Modern Law Review*, 82(1), pp 105–128.

Crewe, T. 2016. The strange death of municipal England. *London Review of Books*, 38(24): 6–10.

Crewe, I. 2020. Authoritarian populism and Brexit in the UK in historical perspective. In *Authoritarian populism and liberal democracy* (pp. 15–31). Basingstoke: Palgrave Macmillan.

Crook, A., Monk, S., Rowley, S. and Whitehead, C. 2006. Planning gain and the supply of new affordable housing in England: understanding the numbers, *Town Planning Review*, 77(3), pp 353–373.

Crosby, N. and Wyatt, P. 2016. Financial viability appraisals for site-specific planning decisions in England, *Environment and Planning C: Government and Policy*, 34(8), pp 1716–1733.

Cutts, D., Goodwin, M., Heath, O. and Surridge, P. 2020. Brexit, the 2019 general election and the realignment of British politics, *The Political Quarterly*.

Davies, A. 2013. 'Right to Buy': the development of a Conservative housing policy, 1945–1980, *Contemporary British History*, 27(4), pp 421–444.

Davies, J.G. 1972. *The evangelistic bureaucrat: A study of a planning exercise in Newcastle upon Tyne*. London: Taylor & Francis.

Davies, G. 2018. The public service gamble: councils borrowing billions to play the property market. www.thebureauinvestigates.com/stories/2018-12-04/councils-borrow-billions-to-buy-real-estate [Accessed 11.03.2020].

Davies, G. 2019. Interest hike for council loans 'could stop regeneration'. www.thebureauinvestigates.com/stories/2019-10-11/interest-hike-for-council-loans-could-stop-regeneration [Accessed 11.03.2020].

DCLG (Department for Communities and Local Government). 2012. National Planning Policy Framework. GOV.UK www.gov.uk/guidance/national-planning-policy-framework [Accessed 18.07.2020].

DCMS. 2018. The Public Services (Social Value) Act 2012. www.gov.uk/government/publications/social-value-act-introductory-guide [Accessed 29.07.2020].

De Graaf, G. and King, M. 1995. Towards a more global government procurement market: the expansion of the GATT Government Procurement Agreement in the context of the Uruguay Round, *International Lawyer*, 29, p 435.

Dixon, R. and Elston, T. 2019. Should councils collaborate? Evaluating shared administration and tax services in English local government, *Public Money & Management*, 39(1), pp 26–36.

Dunleavy, P. 1984. The limits to local government, in *Local socialism?* (pp 49–81). London: Palgrave.

Dunning, R., Inch, A., Payne, S., Watkins, C., While, A., Hickman, H. and Valler, D. 2014. *The impact of the new homes bonus on attitudes and behaviours*. London: DCLG.

Edgerton, D. 2011. War, reconstruction, and the nationalization of Britain, 1939–1951, *Past & Present*, 210(suppl 6), pp 29–46.

Edwards, M. 2016. The housing crisis and London, *City*, 20(2), pp 222–237.

Essex, S. and Brayshay, M. 2008. Boldness diminished? The post-war battle to replan a bomb-damaged provincial city, *Urban History*, 35(3), pp 437–461.

Evans, E.J. 2018. *Thatcher and Thatcherism*. Fourth edition. Abingdon: Routledge.

Fainstein, S. 2016. Financialisation and justice in the city: a commentary, *Urban Studies*, 53(7), pp 1503–1508.

Ferry, L., Andrews, R., Skelcher, C. and Wegorowski, P. 2018. New development: corporatization of local authorities in England in the wake of austerity 2010–2016, *Public Money & Management*, 38(6), pp 477–480.

Findlay-King, L., Nichols, G., Forbes, D. and Macfadyen, G. 2018. Localism and the Big Society: the asset transfer of leisure centres and libraries – fighting closures or empowering communities? *Leisure Studies*, 37(2), pp 158–170.

Finlay, S., Williams, P. and Whitehead, C. 2016. *Evaluation of the Help to Buy Equity Loan Scheme*. London: Department for Communities and Local Government.

Fitzgerald, A. and Lupton, R. 2015. The limits to resilience? The impact of local government spending cuts in London, *Local Government Studies*, 41(4), pp 582–600.

Fitzpatrick, S. and Pawson, H. 2016. Fifty years since Cathy Come Home: critical reflections on the UK homelessness safety net, *International Journal of Housing Policy*, 16(4), pp 543–555.

Floyd, D. 2013. Measuring up: The hidden implication of the Social Value Act. www.youngfoundation.org/social-innovation-investment/measuring-up-the-hidden-implication-of-the-social-value-act/ [Accessed 29.07.2020].

Forrest, R. 2015. The ongoing financialisation of home ownership – new times, new contexts, *International Journal of Housing Policy*, 15(1), pp 1–5.

Forrest, R. and Murie, A. 1983. Residualization and council housing: aspects of the changing social relations of housing tenure, *Journal of Social Policy*, 12(4), pp 453–468.

Forster, M. 2014. *My life in houses*. New York: Vintage.

Foster, M. 2016. Nick Raynsford: Whitehall dismissive of local government abilities. www.publictechnology.net/articles/news/nick-raynsford-whitehall-dismissive-local-government-abilities [Accessed 29.07.2020].

Froud, N. 2018. The Preston Model: municipal socialism or protectionist conjuring trick. Young Fabians blog, 19 November. www.youngfabians.org.uk/the_preston_model_municipal_socialism_or_protectionist_conjuring_trick [Accessed 18.11.2019].

Gains, F. 1999. Implementing privatization policies in 'next steps' agencies, *Public Administration*, 77(4), pp 713–730.

Gallent, N. 2016. Investment, global capital and other drivers of England's housing crisis, *Journal of Urban Regeneration and Renewal*, 9(2), pp 122–138.

Gallent, N., Durrant, D. and May, N. 2017. Housing supply, investment demand and money creation: a comment on the drivers of London's housing crisis, *Urban Studies*, 54(10), pp 2204–2216.

Gallent, N., Durrant, D. and Stirling, P. 2018. Between the unimaginable and the unthinkable: pathways to and from England's housing crisis, *Town Planning Review*, 89(2), pp 125–144.

Gamble, A. 2015. Austerity as statecraft, *Parliamentary Affairs*, 68, pp 42–57.

Garner, J.F. 1979. Policy forum: Skeffington revisited, *Town Planning Review*, 50(4), p 412.

Garside, P.L. 1983. Intergovernmental relations and housing policy in London 1919–1970 with special reference to the density and location of council housing, *The London Journal*, 9(1), pp 39–57.

Gibb, K. 2018. Funding new social and affordable housing. https://housingevidence.ac.uk/wp-content/uploads/2018/11/R2018_SHPWG_funding_models_Ken_Gibb_final.pdf [Accessed 17.12.2019].

Gilbert, B.B. 1965. Health and politics: the British physical deterioration report of 1904, *Bulletin of the History of Medicine*, 39, p 143.

Glasson, J. and Marshall, T. 2007. *Regional planning*. Abingdon: Routledge.

Goss, A. 1961. Neighbourhood units in British new towns, *Town Planning Review*, 32(1), p 66.

Grant Thornton. 2018. In good company: latest trends in local authority trading companies. www.grantthornton.co.uk/globalassets/1.-member-firms/united-kingdom/pdf/search/in-good-company-2018.pdf [Accessed 13.12.2019].

Gray, M., and Barford, A. 2018. The depths of the cuts: The uneven geography of local government austerity. *Cambridge Journal of Regions, Economy and Society*, 11(3), pp 541–563.

Green, J. and Lavery, S. 2018. After neoliberalisation? Monetary indiscipline, crisis and the state, *Transactions of the Institute of British Geographers*, 43, pp 79–94.

Grimshaw, D. 2013. Austerity, privatization and levelling down: Public sector reforms in the United Kingdom. In *Public Sector Shock*. Cheltenham: Edward Elgar Publishing.

Grindrod, J. 2017. *Outskirts: Living life on the edge of the Greenbelt*. London: Sceptre.

Guironnet, A., Attuyer, K., and Halbert, L. 2016. Building cities on financial assets: The financialisation of property markets and its implications for city governments in the Paris city-region. *Urban Studies*, 53(7), pp 1442–1464.

Gurran, N. 2019. *Planning gain: Providing infrastructure and affordable housing*. Chichester: Wiley.

Gurran, N. and Bramley, G. 2017. *Urban planning and the housing market*. Basingstoke: Palgrave Macmillan.

Hackett, P. 2017. *Delivering the renaissance in council-built homes: The rise of local housing companies*. Oxford: The Smith Institute.

Hall, P., Hardy, D., Howard, E. and Ward, C. 2006. *To-morrow: A peaceful path to real reform*. London: Routledge.

Hancock, L. and Mooney, G. 2013. 'Welfare ghettos' and the 'broken society': territorial stigmatization in the contemporary UK, *Housing, Theory and Society*, 30(1), pp 46–64.

Hannah, T.M., Guinan, J. and Bilsborough, J. 2018. The 'Preston Model' and the modern politics of municipal socialism, New Economics, 12 June. https://neweconomics.opendemocracy.net/preston-model-modern-politics-municipal-socialism/ [Accessed 18.11.2019].

Harmon, M. 1997. *The British Labour government and the 1976 IMF crisis*. London: Springer.

Hastings, A. and Bailey, N. 2017. Austerity urbanism in England: the 'regressive redistribution' of local government services and the impact on the poor and marginalised, *Environment and Planning A*, 49(9), pp 2007–2024.

Haworth, A. and Manzi, T. 1999. Managing the 'underclass': interpreting the moral discourse of housing management, *Urban Studies*, 36(1), pp 153–165.

Hays. No date. Oxford City Housing Limited. https://microsites.hays.co.uk/cs/groups/hays_common/@uk/@content/documents/webassets/hays_2552807.pdf [Accessed 11.03.2020].

Hazelton, L.C. 2019. Can applying prefabrication to the UK housing market solve the housing and skills shortages? https://s3.amazonaws.com/academia.edu.documents/60045325/Dissertation_April_201920190718-42781-z3zay9.pdf?response-content-disposition=inline%3B%20filename%3DCan_Applying_Prefabrication_to_the_UK_Ho.pdf&X-Amz-Algorithm=AWS4-HMAC-SHA256&X-Amz-Credential=AKIAIWOWYYGZ2Y53UL3A%2F20200301%2Fus-east-1%2Fs3%2Faws4_request&X-Amz-Date=20200301T124725Z&X-Amz-Expires=3600&X-Amz-SignedHeaders=host&X-Amz-Signature=a793dc3d94eecd20ae9a149a8eadc4a5bce1ac23643ef56aa5f7a0fc56ee60ed

Head, B.W. 2008. Wicked problems in public policy, *Public Policy*, 3(2), p 101.

Healey, P., McNamara, P., Elson, M. and Doak, A. 1988. *Land use planning and the mediation of urban change: The British planning system in practice*. Cambridge: Cambridge University Press.

Hearne, R. 2017. *A home or a wealth generator? Inequality, financialisation and the Irish housing crisis*. Dublin: TASC.

Heim, C.E. 1983. Industrial organisation and regional development in interwar Britain, *The Journal of Economic History*, 43(4), pp 931–952.

Heraud, B. 1973. The new towns: a philosophy of community, *The Sociological Review*, 21(1 suppl), pp 39–55.

Hiber, C. 2013. Help to Buy will likely have the effect of pushing up house prices further, making housing become less–not more– affordable for young would-be-owners, *British Politics and Policy at LSE*. http://eprints.lse.ac.uk/75739/ Accessed 3.12.2019].

Hickson, K. 2005. *The IMF crisis of 1976 and British politics* (Vol. 3). London: IB Tauris.

Hill, D. 2018. Haringey: Council and Lendlease agree settlement over scrapped joint venture scheme. www.onlondon.co.uk/ haringey-council-and-lendlease-agree-settlement-over-scrapped-joint-venture-scheme/ [Accessed 11.03.2020].

HMSO. 1981. *Alternatives to domestic rates*. Cmnd 8449. London: The Stationery Office.

HM Treasury. 2004. Spending Review New public spending plans 2005-2008. London: HM Treasury.

HM Treasury. 2007. Review of sub-national economic development and regeneration London. London: HM Treasury.

HM Treasury. 2020. Budget 2020. www.gov.uk/government/ publications/budget-2020-documents/budget-2020#budget-report [Accessed 13.03.2020].

Hoekman, B. and Mavroidis, P.C. 1995. *The WTO's agreement on government procurement: Expanding disciplines, declining membership?* (No. 1112). CEPR Discussion Papers.

Hollander, G. 2019. How has Haringey moved on from its development vehicle fight? www.insidehousing.co.uk/insight/ insight/how-has-haringey-moved-on-from-its-development-vehicle-fight-61622 [Accessed 11.03.2020].

Holt, G.D., Olomolaiye, P.O. and Harris, F.C. 1995. A review of contractor selection practice in the UK construction industry, *Building and Environment*, 30(4), pp 553–561.

Horner, A. 2017. Town halls buy back Right-to-Buy homes. BBC News, 3 May. www.bbc.co.uk/news/uk-england-39264631 [Accessed 3.12.2019].

Howard, E. 1898. *Tomorrow: a peaceful path to reform*. London: Swan Sonnenschein.

Howard, E. 1902. *Garden Cities of tomorrow*. London: Swan Sonnenschein.

Howard, T., Kuri, L. and Lee, I.P. 2010. September: the Evergreen Cooperative Initiative of Cleveland, Ohio, in *White paper prepared for The Neighborhood Funders Group Annual Conference in Minneapolis, MN.*

Hudak, T.E. 2018. *The Homelessness Reduction Act of 2017.* https://digitalcommons.wpi.edu/mqp-all/2445/ [Accessed 3.12.2019].

Humphreys, I. 1999. Privatisation and commercialisation: changes in UK airport ownership patterns, *Journal of Transport Geography*, 7(2), pp 121–134.

Inlogov 2013. You couldn't make it up – except DCLG just did. https://inlogov.com/tag/jaws-of-doom/ [Accessed 29.07.2020].

Institute for Government. 2019. English devolution: combined authorities and metro mayors. www.instituteforgovernment.org.uk/explainers/english-devolution-combined-authorities-and-metro-mayors [Accessed 11.03.2020].

Ison, S., Francis, G., Humphreys, I. and Page, R. 2011. UK regional airport commercialisation and privatisation: 25 years on, *Journal of Transport Geography*, 19(6), pp 1341–1349.

Jackson, M. and Harrison, L. 2013. *Responding to the Public Services (Social Value) Act 2012.* Manchester: Centre for Local Economic Strategies.

Jennings, J.H. 1971. Geographical implications of the municipal housing programme in England and Wales 1919–39, *Urban Studies*, 8(2), pp 121–138.

Jessop, B., Bonnett, K., Bromley, S. and Ling, T. 1988. *Thatcherism.* Oxford: Basil Blackwell.

John, P. 2014. The great survivor: the persistence and resilience of English local government, *Local Government Studies*, 40(5), pp 687–704.

Johnson, A. 2013. *This boy.* London: Bantam Press.

Jones, C.L. 2018. British cities are moving to reduce the impact of 'studentification'. CityMetric www.citymetric.com/fabric/british-cities-are-moving-reduce-impact-studentification-3659 [Accessed 17.12.2019].

Jones, C. and Murie, A. 2008. *The Right to Buy: Analysis and evaluation of a housing policy* (Vol. 18). Chichester: John Wiley & Sons.

Jones, P. and Comfort, D. 2019. Local authority commercialisation strategies. www.researchgate.net/profile/Peter_Jones46/publication/328922207_A_commentary_on_local_authority_commercialisation_strategies/links/5d81e9c6a6fdcc12cb98ab03/A-commentary-on-local-authority-commercialisation-strategies [Accessed 29.07.2020].

Jordan, E. 2019. *The Wigan Deal: Case study*. Centre for Public Impact. www.centreforpublicimpact.org/case-study/the-wigan-deal/ [Accessed 18.11.2019].

Kelly, J. 2007. The missing ingredient: inter-municipal cooperation and central-local relations in the UK, in Hulst, R., and van Montfort, A., eds, *Inter-municipal cooperation in Europe* (pp 139–210). London: Springer.

Kerr, A. and Radford, M. 1994. TUPE or not TUPE: competitive tendering and the transfer laws, *Public Money & Management*, 14(4), pp 37–45.

Kettle, M. 2020. What the EU procurement furore tells us about Johnson's real priorities. *The Guardian*, 22 April. www.theguardian.com/commentisfree/2020/apr/22/eu-procurement-johnson-priorities-coronavirus-pandemic [Accessed 29.07.2020].

King, P. 2010. *Housing policy transformed: The right to buy and the desire to own*. Bristol: Policy Press.

Kuijper, P.J. 1995. The conclusion and implementation of the Uruguay Round results by the European Community, *European Journal of International Law*, 6, p 222.

Lacey-Barnacle, M. 2019. Exploring local energy justice in times of austerity: civic energy sector low-carbon transitions in Bristol city. PhD thesis, Cardiff University.

Lauermann, J. 2018. Municipal statecraft: revisiting the geographies of the entrepreneurial city, *Progress in Human Geography*, 42(2), pp 205–224.

Letwin, O. 2018 *Independent review of build out: Preliminary update*. London: Cabinet Office.

LB Croydon. 2018. *Suburban design guide*. Croydon: LB Croydon.

LGA (Local Government Association). 2016. *Stronger together: Shared management in local government*. London: LGA.

LGA. 2017a. *Enterprising councils: Supporting councils' income generation activity*. London: LGA.

LGA. 2017b. *Council innovation and learning in housing our homeless households*. London: LGA.

LGA. 2018. *Local government funding: Moving the conversation*. London. LGA.

LGA. 2019a. *Profit with purpose: Delivering social value through commercial activity*. London: LGA.

LGA. 2019b. Housing Revenue Account cap removal: survey results. www.local.gov.uk/sites/default/files/documents/Publications%20-%20Research%20-%20Housing%20Revenue%20Account%20Cap%20Removal%20-%20Survey%20Results%20-%20March%202019.pdf [Accessed 11.03.2020].

LGA and NHF (Local Government Association and National Housing Federation). 2019. *Housing associations and councils working together to end homelessness*. London: LGA.

LGiU and MJ. 2020. *State of Local Government Finance Survey 2020*. London: LGiU.

Loopstra, R., Reeves, A., Barr, B., Taylor-Robinson, D., McKee, M. and Stuckler, D. 2016. The impact of economic downturns and budget cuts on homelessness claim rates across 323 local authorities in England, 2004–12, *Journal of Public Health*, 38(3), pp 417–425.

London Councils. 2019. *The cost of homelessness services in London*. London: London Councils.

Low, N. 1983. Spatial equity and housing policy, *Local Government Studies*, 9(2), pp 35–49.

Lowndes, V. and Gardner, A. 2016. Local governance under the Conservatives: super-austerity, devolution and the 'smarter state', *Local Government Studies*, 42(3), pp 357–375.

Lowndes, V. and McCaughie, K. 2013. Weathering the perfect storm? Austerity and institutional resilience in local government, *Policy & Politics*, 41(4), pp 533–549.

Lunn, E. 2019. Britain's Independent councillors face challenges of success. Money Week, 27 March. https://moneyweek.com/503652/investing-in-student-property-doesnt-stack-up/ [Accessed 17.12. 2019].

Majeed, A. and Buckman, L. 2016. Should all GPs become NHS employees? *BMJ*, 355, p i5064.

Malpass, P. 2000. The discontinuous history of housing associations in England, *Housing Studies*, 15(2), pp 195–212.

Malpass, P. 2005. *Housing and the welfare state: The development of housing policy in Britain*. Basingstoke: Palgrave Macmillan.

Malpass, P. and Mullins, D. 2002. Local authority housing stock transfer in the UK: from local initiative to national policy, *Housing Studies*, 17(4), pp 673–686.

Marmot, M. 2020. Health equity in England: The Marmot review 10 years on. *BMJ*, 368.

Marsh, P.T. and Gordon, Jr, J.L. 1995. Joseph Chamberlain: entrepreneur in politics, *History: Reviews of New Books*, 24(1), pp 3–4.

May, T. 2018. Making housing fairer, Speech by Theresa May. www.insidehousing.co.uk/insight/insight/mays-planning-speech-in-full-55056 [Accessed 28.07.2020].

Maynard, A. 1991. Developing the health care market, *The Economic Journal*, 101(408), pp 1277–1286.

Mayor of London. 2018. Homebuilding capacity fund. www.london.gov.uk/what-we-do/housing-and-land/homebuilding-capacity-fund [Accessed 13.03.2020].

McAdam, R. and Walker, T. 2004. Evaluating the best value framework in UK local government services, *Public Administration and Development: The International Journal of Management Research and Practice*, 24(3), pp 183–196.

McAfee, R.P. and McMillan, J. 1989. Government procurement and international trade, *Journal of International Economics*, 26(3–4), pp 291–308.

McAllister, P., Shepherd, E. and Wyatt, P. 2018. Policy shifts, developer contributions and land value capture in London 2005–2017, *Land Use Policy*, 78, pp 316–326.

McAllister, P., Street, E. and Wyatt, P. 2016. Governing calculative practices: an investigation of development viability modelling in the English planning system, *Urban Studies*, 53(11), pp 2363–2379.

McCrone, G. and Stephens, M. 2017. *Housing policy in Britain and Europe*. Abingdon: Routledge.

McCurdy, C., Gardiner, L., Gustafsson, M. and Handscomb, K. 2020. *Painting the towns blue: Demography, economy and living standards in the political geographies emerging from the 2019 general election*. London: Resolution Foundation.

McDonald, M. 1997. The impact of the plan-led system, *Journal of Planning and Environment Law Occasional Papers*, 25, pp 45–50.

McKee, K. 2010. The end of the Right to Buy and the future of social housing in Scotland, *Local Economy*, 25(4), pp 319–327.

McKee, K., Muir, J. and Moore, T. 2016. Housing policy in the UK: the importance of spatial nuance, *Housing Studies*, 32(1), pp 60–72.

McPhillips, M. 2017. *The impact of homelessness on children and their development*. London: Shelter.

Melhuish, E., Belsky, J. and Barnes, J. 2010. Evaluation and value of Sure Start, *Archives of Disease in Childhood*, 95(3), pp 159–161.

MHCLG (Ministry of Housing, Communities and Local Government). 2017. *Fixing our broken housing market*. London: MHCLG.

MHCLG. 2018a. Use of receipts from Right to Buy sales: consultation. https://assets.publishing.service.gov.uk/government/uploads/ system/uploads/attachment_data/file/733469/Right_to_Buy_ consultation.pdf [Accessed 11.03.2020].

MHCLG. 2018b. Clarification on proposed changes: Q&A. www. gov.uk/government/consultations/proposed-changes-to-the-prudential-framework-of-capital-finance/prudential-framework-of-capital-finance-qa [Accessed 11.03.2020].

MHCLG. 2018c. A new deal for social housing. https://assets. publishing.service.gov.uk/government/uploads/system/uploads/ attachment_data/file/733605/A_new_deal_for_social_housing_ web_accessible.pdf [Accessed 29.07.2020].

MHCLG. 2019a. *National design guide*. London: MHCLG.

MHCLG. 2019b. Affordable housing supply: April 2018 to March 2019 England. https://assets.publishing.service.gov.uk/ government/uploads/system/uploads/attachment_data/file/ 847661/Affordable_Housing_Supply_2018-19.pdf [Accessed 11.03.2020].

MHCLG 2019c. *National Planning Policy Framework*. MHCLG. Live tables. www.gov.uk/government/statistical-data-sets/live-tables-on-house-building [Accessed 29.07.2020].

Monbiot, G. 2020. Tory privatisation is at the heart of the UK's disastrous coronavirus response, *The Guardian*, 27 May.

Moor, F. and Sandford, M. 2017. *Local Economy*, 32(5), pp 399–419.

Morphet, J. 2003. New towns in the novel: a reflection on social realism, *Planning Practice & Research*, 18(1), pp 51–62.

Morphet, J. 2004. The role of the community strategy, *Town and Country Planning*, pp 164–165.

Morphet, J. 2007. *Modern local government*. London: Sage.

Morphet, J. 2011. *Effective practice in spatial planning*. Abingdon: Routledge.

Morphet, J. 2016. Local authorities build again. *Town and Country Planning*, March, pp 170–177.

Morphet, J. 2017. *Combined authorities–the next big thing? Town and Country Planning*, March, pp 96–103.

Morphet, J. 2018. *Top down or bottom up? How subsidiarity is helping local authorities change the government's supply side housing policies*. London: Political Studies Association.

Morphet, J. and Clifford, B. 2017. *Local authority direct delivery of housing*. London: NPF and RTPI.

Morphet J. and Clifford, B. 2019. *Local authority direct delivery of housing: 2019 continuation report*. London: RTPI.

Morrison, N. and Burgess, G. 2014. Inclusionary housing policy in England: the impact of the downturn on the delivery of affordable housing through Section 106, *Journal of Housing and the Built Environment*, 29(3), pp 423–438.

Morton, A. 2010. *Making housing affordable*. London: Policy Exchange.

Morton, A. 2016. *How to deliver a one nation housing policy*. London: Conservative Home.

Moulaert, F., Martinelli, F., Swyngedouw, E. and Gonzalez, S. 2005. Towards alternative model(s) of local innovation, *Urban Studies*, 42(11), pp 1969–1990.

Mullins, D., Murie, A. and Leather, P. 2006. *Housing policy in the UK*. Basingstoke: Palgrave.

Murie, A. 2016. *The Right to Buy? Selling off public and social housing*. Bristol: Policy Press.

Murphy, L. 2018. *The invisible land: The hidden force driving the UK's unequal economy and broken housing market*. London: IPPR Commission on Economic Justice.

NAO (National Audit Office). 2014. Financial sustainability of local authorities. London: NAO.

NAO. 2016. *Financial sustainability of local authorities: Capital expenditure and resourcing*. London: NAO.

NAO. 2017a. *Short guide to local government*. London: NAO.

NAO. 2017b. *Homelessness*. London: NAO.

NAO. 2017c. *Housing in England: Overview*. London: NAO.

NAO. 2018. *Financial sustainability of local authorities 2018*. London: NAO.

NAO. 2019. *Local authority governance*. London: NAO.

NAO. 2020. *Local authority investment in commercial property*. London: NAO.

Nay, O., Béjean, S., Benamouzig, D., Bergeron, H., Castel, P. and Ventelou, B. 2016. Achieving universal health coverage in France: policy reforms and the challenge of inequalities, *The Lancet*, 387(10034), pp 2236–2249.

Naylor, C. and Wellings, D. 2019. *A citizen-led approach to health and care: Lessons from the Wigan Deal*. London: The King's Fund.

Needham, C. and Mangan, C. 2014. *The 21st century public servant*. Birmingham: University of Birmingham.

O'Brien, P. and Pike, A. 2015. City deals, decentralisation and the governance of local infrastructure funding and financing in the UK, *National Institute Economic Review*, 233(1), pp R14–R26.

O'Brien, P., Pike, A. and Tomaney, J. 2019. Governing the 'ungovernable'? Financialisation and the governance of transport infrastructure in the London 'global city-region', *Progress in Planning*, 132, pp 1004–1022.

ODPM (Office of the Deputy Prime Minister). 2001. *Planning: Delivering fundamental change*. London: ODPM.

OECD (Organisation for Economic Co-operation and Development). 2017. *Subnational governments in OECD countries key data*. 2018 edition. Paris: OECD.

Olechnowicz, A. 1997. *Working-class housing in England between the wars: The Becontree Estate*. Oxford: Oxford University Press.

Orr, K. and Vince, R. 2009. Traditions of local government, *Public Administration*, 87(3), pp 655–677.

Overmans, J. and Noordegraaf, M. 2014. Managing austerity: rhetorical and real responses to fiscal stress in local government, *Public Money & Management*, 34(2), pp 99–106.

Painter, J. 1991. Compulsory competitive tendering in local government: the first round, *Public Administration*, 69(2), pp 191–210.

Paris, C. and Frey, J. 2018. Demographic trends and changing housing systems in Northern Ireland, *Housing Studies*, 33(8), pp 1264–1285.

Parker, D. 2009. *The official history of privatization: Volume 1: The formative years 1970–1987*. Abingdon: Routledge.

Pearson, C. and Delatte, N. 2005. Ronan Point apartment tower collapse and its effect on building codes, *Journal of Performance of Constructed Facilities*, 19(2), pp 172–177.

Penny, J. 2017. Between coercion and consent: the politics of 'cooperative governance' at a time of 'austerity localism' in London, *Urban Geography*, 38(9), pp 1352–1373.

Phelps, N. and Miao, J. 2019. 'Varieties of urban entrepreneurialism', *Dialogues in Human Geography*.

Pike, A., O'Brian, P., Stickland, T., Thrower, G. and Tomaney, J. 2019. *Financialising city statecraft and infrastructure*. Cheltenham: Edward Elgar.

Place Alliance 2020. A housing design audit for England. http://placealliance.org.uk/research/national-housing-audit/ [Accessed 29.07.2020].

Porter, M. 2010. Anchor institutions and urban economic development: from community benefit to shared value, in *Inner City Economic Forum Summit 2010*.

Raco, M., Parker, G. and Doak, J. 2006. Reshaping spaces of local governance? Community strategies and the modernisation of local government in England, *Environment and Planning C: Government and Policy*, 24(4), pp 475–496.

Raven, J. ed. 2015. *Lost mansions: Essays on the destruction of the country house.* London: Springer.

Reeves, P. 2006. *Introduction to social housing.* London: Routledge.

Rhodes, R.A.W. 2018. *Control and power in central-local government relations.* Abingdon: Routledge.

Ridley, N. 1991. *My style of government: The Thatcher years.* London: Hutchinson.

Rodríguez-Pose, A. 2018. The revenge of the places that don't matter (and what to do about it), *Cambridge Journal of Regions, Economy and Society*, 11, pp 189–209.

Rowe, J.K., Peredo, A.M., Sullivan, M. and Restakis, J. 2017. Cooperative development, policy, and power in a period of contested neoliberalism: the case of Evergreen Cooperative Corporation in Cleveland, Ohio, *Socialist Studies*, 12(1), pp 54–77.

Ryan-Collins, J. 2019. Breaking the housing–finance cycle: macroeconomic policy reforms for more affordable homes, *Environment and Planning A.*

Sandford, M. 2016. Public services and local government: the end of the principle of 'funding following duties', *Local Government Studies*, 42(4), pp 637–656.

Sandford, M. 2017. The quiet return of equalization alongside incentive in the English local government finance system, *Public Money & Management*, 37(4), pp 245–252.

Sandford, M. 2019a. *Local government: Commercial property investments.* House of Commons Library Briefing Paper. Number 08142.

Sandford, M. 2019b. *One public estate.* London: House of Commons Library debate pack. 13 May.

Sandford, M. 2020. *Devolution to local government in England.* London: House of Commons Library.

Saugeres, L. 2000. Of tidy gardens and clean houses: housing officers as agents of social control, *Geoforum*, *31*(4), pp 587–599.

Savage, M. 2019. Ministers urged to halt right-to-buy scheme More than 40% of former council homes now rented out by private landlords, *The Guardian*, 19 January. www.theguardian.com/society/2019/jan/19/ministers-urged-halt-right-buy-council-homes-rented [Accessed 17.12.2019].

Schwartz, J.D. 2009. In Cleveland, worker co-ops look to a Spanish model, *Time*, 22 December.

Scott, P. 2001. Industrial estates and British industrial development, 1897–1939, *Business History*, 43(2), pp 73–98.

Scott, P. and Walsh, P. 2004. Patterns and determinants of manufacturing plant location in interwar London, *The Economic History Review*, 57(1), pp 109–141.

Seldon, A. and Collings, D. 2014. *Britain under Thatcher*. London: Routledge.

Semple, A. 2012. Reform of the EU procurement directives and WTO GPA: Forward steps for sustainability? Available at SSRN 2089357.

SEUK (Social Enterprise UK). 2019. *Front and centre: Putting social value at the heart of inclusive growth*. London: SEUK.

Shaw, G.B. 1892. *Widowers' Houses*. Play.

Sheail, J. 1979. The Restriction of Ribbon Development Act: the character and perception of land-use control in inter-war Britain, *Regional Studies*, 13(6), pp 501–512.

Sheppard, A. and Smith, N. 2011. Delivering homes and infrastructure through incentivisation: the role of the growth points agenda and the New Homes Bonus. https://uwe-repository.worktribe.com/output/960009 [Accessed 21.11.2019].

Shipman, A. 2015. The Conservative Manifesto – then and now. www.open.edu/openlearn/people-politics-law/the-conservative-manifesto-then-and-now [Accessed 29.07.2020].

Shrubsole, G. 2018. How the extent of county farms has halved in 40 years. Who Owns England, 8 June. https://whoownsengland.org/2018/06/08/how-the-extent-of-county-farms-has-halved-in-40-years/ [Accessed 11.12.2019].

Shrubsole, G. 2019. *Who owns England? How we lost our green and pleasant land, and how to take it back*. London: HarperCollins UK.

Simcock, T. and McKee, K. 2019. Landlords will be forbidden from evicting tenants for no reason–but reform has only just begun. *The Conversation*. www.storre.stir.ac.uk/retrieve/19c93c94-0591-4019-b74e-b6413eecfae3/McKee-Conversation-2019.pdf [Accessed 3.12.2019].

Skeffington, F. 1969. *People and planning*. London: HMSO.

Skelcher, C. 2017. An enterprising municipality? Municipalisation, corporatisation and the political economy of Birmingham City Council in the nineteenth and twenty-first centuries, *Local Government Studies*, 43(6), pp 927–945.

Skidmore, C. 2017. Birmingham municipal housing trust: delivering new homes for rent, sale and the private rented sector. Presentation delivered to RTPI-NPF report launch event, London.

Smith, B. 2018. *Social housing in Wales*. London: UK Collaborative Centre for Housing Evidence.

Smith Institute. 2018. *The hidden costs of poor quality housing in the north*. Oxford: Smith Institute.

Smulian, M. 2019. Bigger picture, *The Planner*, April, pp 23–25.

Solesbury, W. 2013. *Policy in urban planning: Structure plans, programmes and local plans* (Vol. 8). London: Elsevier.

Spencer, K. 1995. The reform of social housing, in Stewart, J., and Stoker, G., eds, *Local government in the 1990s* (pp 145–165). London: Springer.

Stevenson, J. 1991. The Jerusalem that failed? The rebuilding of post-war Britain, in Gourvish, T., and O'Day, O., eds, *Britain since 1945* (pp 89–110). Basingstoke: Palgrave.

Stoker, G. 1988. *The politics of British local government*. London: Macmillan.

Stoker, G. 1997. Hearing but not listening: the local government review process, *Public Administration*, 75(1), pp 35–48.

Stone, J. 2020. Boris Johnson says austerity 'certainly not part' of government's economic response to coronavirus, *The Independent*, 30 April.

Strong, R., Binney, M., Harris, J. and Harris, J. 1974. *The destruction of the country house, 1875–1975*. London: Thames and Hudson.

Swenarton, M. 2018. *Homes fit for heroes: The politics and architecture of early state housing in Britain*. London: Routledge.

T'Hart, P. and Boin, A. 2001. Between crisis and normalcy: The long shadow of post-crisis politics, in Rosenthal, U., Boin, A., and Comfort, L., eds, *Managing crises: Threats, dilemmas, opportunities* (pp 28–46). Springfield, IL: Charles C. Thomas.

Taylor-Gooby, P. 2012. Root and branch restructuring to achieve major cuts: the social policy programme of the 2010 UK coalition government, *Social Policy & Administration*, 46(1), pp 61–82.

Tewdwr-Jones, M., Morphet, J. and Allmendinger, P. 2006. The contested strategies of local governance: community strategies, development plans, and local government modernisation, *Environment and Planning A*, 38(3), pp 533–551.

Theakston, K. 1995. *The civil service since 1945*. London: Blackwell.

The Planner. 2018. Backlog of more than 400,000 homes with permission, says LGA. The Planner. www.theplanner.co.uk/news/backlog-of-more-than-400000-homes-with-permission-says-lga [Accessed 11.03.2020].

Thompson, M. 2020. What's so new about new municipalism?, *Progress in Human Geography*, first published online 9 March 2020. https://journals.sagepub.com/doi/full/10.1177/0309132520909480 [Accessed 18.07.2020].

Thompson, M., Nowak V., Southern, A., Davies, J. and Furmedge, P. 2020. Re-grounding the city with Polanyi: from urban entrepreneurialism to entrepreneurial municipalism, *Environment and Planning A: Economy and Space*, first published online 9 January 2020. https://journals.sagepub.com/doi/full/10.1177/0308518X19899698 [Accessed 18.07.2020].

Thompson, M. (2020). What's so new about new municipalism? *Progress in Human Geography*. doi:10.1177/0309132520909480.

Tighe, C. and Bounds, A. 2019. Britain's Independent councillors face challenges of success, *Financial Times*, 14 May.

Todd, S. 2019. *Tastes of honey: The making of Shelagh Delaney and a cultural revolution*. New York: Vintage.

Tomkinson, R. 2017. *Shared services in local government: Improving service delivery*. London: Routledge.

Toynbee, P. and Walker D. 2020 *The Lost Decade: 2010–2020, and What Lies Ahead for Britain*. Guardian Faber.

Travers, T. 2015. *London boroughs at 50*. London: Biteback.

Turner, J. 2014. *Macmillan*. Abingdon: Routledge.

UK Debt Management Office. *Public Works Loan Board Annual Report and Accounts 2018–2019*. London: UKDMO.

Vaughan, A. 2019. Dutch eco initiative halves energy bills in first UK homes, *The Guardian*, 7 January. www.theguardian.com/society/2019/jan/07/dutch-eco-homes-idea-arrives-in-uk-and-cuts-energy-bills-in-half-nottingham-energiesprong [Accessed 12.03.2020].

Wainwright, O. 2019a. Meet the councils quietly building a housing revolution, *The Guardian*, 28th October. www.theguardian.com/cities/2019/oct/28/meet-the-councils-quietly-building-a-housing-revolution [Accessed 17.12.2019].

Wainwright, O. 2019b. 'A masterpiece': Norwich council houses win Stirling architecture prize, *The Guardian*, 8 October. www.theguardian.com/artanddesign/2019/oct/08/stirling-prize-architecture-goldsmith-street-norwich-council-houses [Accessed 11.03.2020].

Waite, D., Maclennan, D. and O'Sullivan, T. 2013. Emerging city policies: devolution, deals and disorder, *Local Economy*, 28(7–8), pp 770–785.

Walsh, K. 1995. *Public services and market mechanisms: Competition, contracting and the New Public Management*. London: Macmillan.

Walters, T 1918. *Report of the Committee to consider questions of building construction in connection with dwellings for the working classes*. London: The Stationery Office.

Ward, K., Newman, J., John, P., Theodore, N., Macleavy, J. and Cochrane, A. 2015. Whatever happened to local government? A review symposium, *Regional Studies, Regional Science*, 2(1), pp 435–457.

Ward, M. 2019. *Local growth deals*. Briefing SNO 7120. London: House of Commons Library.

Ward, S.V. 1990. Local industrial promotion and development policies 1899–1940, *Local Economy*, 5(2), pp 100–118.

Watermeyer, R. 2004. *Project synthesis report: Unpacking transparency in government procurement–rethinking WTO Government Procurement Agreements*. London: CUTS Centre for International Trade, Economics and Environment, Unpacking Transparency in Government Procurement, pp 1–50.

Watt, P. and Minton, A. 2016. London's housing crisis and its activisms, *City*, 20(2), pp 204–221.

White, C.W. 2018. "The foundations of the national glory are in the homes of the people": the Addison Act, the First World War, and British housing policy. Doctoral dissertation, University of Oxford.

White, J. 2016a. *London in the nineteenth century: 'A human awful wonder of God'*. London: Random House.

White, J. 2016b. *London in the twentieth century: A city and its people*. London: Random House.

Whitehead, C. and Williams, P. 2011. Causes and consequences? Exploring the shape and direction of the housing system in the UK post the financial crisis, *Housing Studies*, 26(7–8), pp 1157–1169.

Whyte, W.F. and Whyte, K.K. 2014. *Making Mondragon: The growth and dynamics of the worker cooperative complex*. New York: Cornell University Press.

Wigan Council. 2019. The Deal. www.wigan.gov.uk/council/the-deal/the-deal.aspx [Accessed 18.11.2019].

Wilding, P. 1973. The Housing and Town Planning Act 1919—a study in the making of social policy, *Journal of Social Policy*, 2(4), pp 317–334.

Williams, A. 2018. Haringey Council scraps £4bn property venture with Lendlease, *Financial Times*, 18 July. www.ft.com/content/1b3c6798-8a84-11e8-b18d-0181731a0340 [Accessed 11.03.2020].

Williams, P.M. 2002. Community strategies: mainstreaming sustainable development and strategic planning?. *Sustainable Development*, 10(4), pp 197–205.

Wills, J. 2016. *Locating localism statecraft, citizenship and democracy*. Bristol: Policy Press.

Wilson, A. 1964. *Late call*. London: Faber and Faber.

Wilson, J.F. 1991. Ownership, management and strategy in early north-west gas companies, *Business History*, 33(2), pp 203–221.

Wilson, W. 2015. *The New Homes Bonus scheme*. London: House of Commons Library.

Wilson, W. and Barton, C. 2019. *Statutory homelessness in England*. Briefing Paper Number 01164. London: House of Commons Library.

Wyatt, P. 2018. Can land value uplift deliver affordable housing? Experiences from England, *Journal of European Real Estate Research*, 11(1), pp 87–101.

Young, K. and Garside, P.L. 1982. *Metropolitan London, politics and urban change, 1837–1981* (Vol. 6). New York: Holmes & Meier.

Index

Ministry of Housing,
  Communities and Local
  Government 20, 54, 65–66, 69,
  75, 99, 126–127
mobility 31
Mondragon 90
Monk, S. 53, 63
Morphet, J. 34, 42, 47, 51, 52, 54,
  87, 89, 93, 132
Morphet, J. and Clifford, B. 20–
  22, 32, 49, 54, 60, 66, 88, 143
mortgage finance 18, 24–25, 98
municipal entrepreneurialism 26,
  29–32, 85, 94, 100, 101, 133,
  135, 141–142, 144
Murie, Alan 19, 44, 48, 55

N

National Audit Office 1, 4, 5, 9,
  11–19, 21, 67, 81, 92, 98, 124,
  132, 135
National Planning Policy
  Framework (NPPF) *see*
  planning system
Neoliberalism 17, 27, 29,
  141, 143
Netherlands 8, 74, 113
New Homes Bonus 11, 16, 53, 84
New Public Management 9
new towns 50
Newcastle upon Tyne,
  Metropolitan Borough 12
NHS *see* health
Noordegraaf, M. 8, 14, 17
North West 102
Northamptonshire 10, 12
Northern Ireland 25, 34
Norwich, District Council 111
Nottingham 92, 96, 101, 112, 130
Nottingham, Unitary
  Authority 92, 96, 101, 112

O

OECD 3, 43, 83, 131, 133
older people 5, 29, 56, 63, 90–91,
  110–112
One Public Estate 79, 119
Osborne, G. 121, 131

out county estates 37
outsourcing 14, 47, 55–56, 67, 74,
  86, 92–94, 96, 99, 108; *see also*
  liberalisation
Overmans, J. 8, 14, 17
owner occupiers 18
Oxford, District Council 41,
  95, 105

P

parks 15, 31
Passivhaus 111
Penny, J. 5, 7, 10, 12, 16, 141
  Beswick and Penny 22, 27, 28,
  29, 37, 71, 139, 142
permitted development 22, 67–69
Peterborough, Unitary
  Authority 96
Phelps, N. and Miao, J. 29, 90, 97,
  140, 142, 143
Pike, A. 26, 27, 83
place alliance 69
places 2, 5–6, 11–12, 26, 29,
  34–35, 61, 64–65, 71, 91, 94,
  96, 123
planning committee 70
Planning and Compulsory
  Purchase Act 2004 52
planning control 6, 23
planning gain 22
planning reform 25, 51, 124
planning system 21, 50–59, 66,
  69, 129, 136–137
  clawback 63, 70
  local plans 2, 50–53, 62, 69, 86,
  110, 138
  National Planning Policy
  Framework 49, 53, 64, 66,
  124–125
  Section 106, 64–65, 69–70, 77,
  80, 105–106, 110, 116
Plymouth, Unitary Authority 128
poverty 11, 22, 35, 55–56,
  110, 112
Preston, District Council 85, 90–
  91, 121, 128
private rent 19, 49, 101, 113,
  117–118, 127